ICE CREAM

AN IRRESISTIBLE HISTORY

ROBIN DAVIS HEIGEL

Charleston | London

THE
History
PRESS

Published by The History Press
Charleston, SC 29403
www.historypress.net

Copyright © 2010 by Robin Davis Heigel
All rights reserved

First published 2010

Manufactured in the United States
ISBN 978.1.59629.971.9

Library of Congress Cataloging-in-Publication Data

Heigel, Robin Davis.
Graeter's Ice Cream : an irresistible history / Robin Davis Heigel.
p. cm.
Includes bibliographical references and index.
ISBN 978-1-59629-971-9
1. Graeter's (Firm)--History. 2. Ice cream industry--United States--History. 3.
Ice cream parlors--Ohio--Cincinnati--History I. Title.
HD9281.U54G734 2010
338.7'63740973--dc22
2010019124

CONTENTS

FOREWORD

The ancient Greek tragedians taught that only through suffering can one gain wisdom. Perhaps this is why most family businesses do not make it to the fourth generation. The succeeding generations, thanks to the hard work of the prior ones, do not have to work so hard to enjoy the good life, and so they lose the entrepreneurial zeal and dedication that gives all great family businesses an edge over their big-business competition. In such cases, the latter generations eventually run down their legacy or sell out—usually both. Thankfully, my family has steadfastly been able to avoid this fate. So maybe a little suffering is not such a bad thing! I guess that makes yet one more thing I owe to my father. Thanks, Dad!

As every family business consultant and advice book will tell you, the most dangerous and painful road that all family businesses must negotiate is transitioning from one generation to the next. My family has certainly had its share of pain during its transitions over the years. An untimely death, an irreconcilable feud between brothers, a debilitating accident, bickering cousins and a near-death experience—all these and more marked the transitions of one generation to another for the Graeter family.

And yet through it all, we have survived and come out stronger, I think, thanks to the one shared value that we all hold dear above all other things: the quality of our product, Graeter's Ice Cream. Over the years, the family has probably disagreed on everything under the sun. But we have never disagreed on our dedication to quality. And that has been the glue that has kept us together for over 140 years.

When asked if I regret the struggle with the difficult transition to our generation, I reply that I do not. Had it been easy, then perhaps my cousins and I would not have the strong partnership that we now enjoy. It has been said that such bonds form among those who share a traumatic experience. We certainly had our share of trauma trying to figure out how to move to the fourth generation, but I can honestly say that the relationship among us, and with our aunt and fathers, has never been stronger. The ancients were right: wisdom comes through suffering. May heaven help the upcoming fifth generation!

What follows is a story about our family, our business and, most importantly, our ice cream. We have seen many changes over the years and have made many changes, but we have never sacrificed on our core promise: to simply make the best ice cream that you'll ever taste. Readers of bestselling business author (and my personal favorite) Jim Collins will readily understand this precept.

At one time, everyone made ice cream the way we do. Now, we are the only ones left. Why? Because we always understood that we must never change the product, a fact that liberated us to make other changes necessary to survive through fourteen decades.

The other reason we're the only ones still making ice cream the old-fashioned way? Because the Graeter family is just that darn stubborn.

Richard A. Graeter II
President and CEO of Graeter's Inc.and
Graeter's Manufacturing Company
Fourth generation of Graeter family

ACKNOWLEDGEMENTS

I created this book primarily from interviews with the Graeter family. Dick, Lou and Kathy gave me their recollections of their father, grandfather and the earliest years of the business, while Richard and Chip detailed what it was like to grow up as a Graeter and the difficult transition to becoming the owners of the company. I supplemented the family information with historical information from books, newspapers and magazine articles and various online sources, including timeline.org, as noted in the bibliography.

My thanks go out to the Graeter family for being so open with me about their family history and for helping me piece together the different eras. Thanks especially to Richard, who went through the manuscript carefully to make sure the details I had collected from so many different sources were correct.

I would also like to thank Joe Gartrell and The History Press for the opportunity to write this book.

To my friends and family, thank you for accompanying me on multiple trips to Graeter's Ice Cream every time I needed a break from research and writing to get some sweet inspiration. I know it was a sacrifice. I wish my jeans had been as accommodating as all of you.

And I would like to offer a special thank-you to my family. Ben, thanks for being understanding when I needed to miss so many of your tennis matches to finish the book. Molly and Sarah, thanks for putting up with so many nights of "grab-and-go" dinners.

I would also like to give my biggest thanks to my husband, Ken, for his photographic contributions to the book, for careful and kind editing of the words and for his constant encouragement.

INTRODUCTION

Historians do not agree on when or where ice cream was created, but the general consensus is that it was invented in China in the form of sweet ice, possibly as early as 3000 BC. Centuries later, Marco Polo discovered it on his world travels, and he then supposedly took the treat back to Italy, where it was made into something closer to what we now call "ice cream."

While this can't be confirmed or denied, it is certain that the ice cream enjoyed in the United States today came from Europe. Thomas Jefferson, who ate ice cream in France, is credited with making it popular in America. The Jefferson Papers Collection at the Library of Congress houses one of the first printed recipes for ice cream, from 1784. It calls simply for cream, sugar and eggs and was made using a machine called the sabottiere or sorbetiere, which looks like a primitive version of today's hand-cranked ice cream makers.

From there, ice cream became the darling of anyone who had some version of a maker and access to ice. The rich treat had to be cranked and enjoyed right away, because without refrigerators or freezers, there was no means of storing it frozen for any length of time.

In the late 1800s in Cincinnati, Ohio, Louis Charles Graeter turned to ice cream to make a living. He cranked the ice cream in the back room of the bottom floor of his home on McMillan Street and sold it out the front. He used what was known as the "French pot," a spinning bowl that would throw the sweet mixture against the sides, from where he scraped it as it froze, not much different than the early sabottieire.

Now, almost 150 years later, an ice cream produced by the fourth generation of the Graeter family—in virtually the same manner—is considered by many to be one of the best ice creams in the country. It has gained national notoriety, being highlighted in *O!* magazine and featured in other publications such as *Gourmet, Vanity Fair* and *Saveur*. Mystery writer James Patterson included Graeter's Ice Cream in one of his thrillers, *Honeymoon*, in 2005.

Ohio senator Gary Cates used Graeter's Ice Cream to sweeten the pot, so to speak, feeding it to other senators in order to get a bill on workman's compensation passed in 2005. "I found that people are a lot friendlier when they're eating Graeter's Ice Cream," Cates said in an article in the *Columbus Dispatch*.

In Ohio, Graeter's Ice Cream represents such a part of the fabric of life that it is not uncommon to find obituaries that list the ice cream among the favorite things of the deceased, along with the Cincinnati Reds and the Ohio State Buckeyes.

Graeter's Ice Cream is no ordinary ice cream, though the flavors certainly sound familiar and it can be found somewhere as ordinary as a supermarket freezer in certain parts of the country. Graeter's is more than just a pleasant regional ice cream, like Pierre's of Cleveland with its dozens of flavors or Velvet Ice Cream of Utica, Ohio, even though Velvet is also family owned and almost as old as Graeter's. And Graeter's is different than the new breed of artisan ice creams, such as Jeni's Splendid Ice Creams in Columbus, with its far-out flavors. The flavors at Graeter's have changed little in the last seventy-five years.

Graeter's is, by and large, exactly the same as it was when Louis Charles hand stirred it in the original French pots. There's a lot to be said for a product that has maintained such consistency and such a loyal following for that length of time. And the company is still 100 percent family owned, no small feat considering that less than 3 percent of family businesses survive into the fourth generation.

The company's history encompasses a story of love and division, bickering and communing, but always with attention to one of the most irresistible products in America: its ice cream.

How sweet is that?

THE EARLY YEARS

People have called Cincinnati many names: Porkopolis, Queen of the West, Queen City, Blue Chip City and the City of Seven Hills. But the city along the Ohio River that was founded in 1788 got its final name from a famous ancient Roman general named Cincinnatus. Many considered Cincinnatus, who lived roughly from 520 to 430 BC, to be a hero for defeating the Aequians, Sabinians and Volscians— and then resigning from the dictatorship he had rightly won to rule only his own farm.

Cincinnati resembled pioneer-era cities such as Pittsburgh and Nashville, riverboat towns like St. Louis and New Orleans and immigrant-industrial metropolises similar to Brooklyn, Philadelphia, Chicago and Detroit.

Cincinnati consisted of a large area, with the Ohio River forming the southern boundary and the hills to the north enclosing its basin. Initially, people and businesses set up in the basin of the city, near the river, because it could be harnessed for energy and transportation of goods and people.

The introduction of steam navigation on the Ohio River and the completion of the Miami and Erie Canal helped the city's population grow. The city limits stopped at Liberty Street, and the area above it was known as the Northern Liberties because it was not subject to the laws of the city. As such, it drew a concentration of bootleggers, saloons and entrepreneurs. In 1848, the city annexed the area as its first "suburb."

The city considered itself a jewel of the Midwest, and to prove it, it held industrial expositions every year from 1870 to 1888 to showcase invention, trade and the arts. These gatherings proved that Cincinnati was a center of music, art and industry.

Cincinnati was one of the first American cities to be home to a zoo. The Zoological Society of Cincinnati was founded in 1873 and officially opened the gates to the Cincinnati Zoo & Botanical Garden in 1875. At the time, its animal collection was very small: just a few monkeys, grizzly bears, deer, raccoons and elk but an impressive collection of birds, including a talking crow.

The city also played home to a professional baseball team: the Red Stockings who eventually went on to become simply, the Reds. In their first season in 1869, they went undefeated.

The city became an important stop along the Underground Railroad in the pre–Civil War era because it bordered on the slave state of Kentucky. Historical papers often mention Cincinnati as a crucial stopping place for those escaping slavery.

During the eighteenth and nineteenth centuries, public markets represented the primary source for buying and selling perishable food in Cincinnati, as they were in other urban centers. Butchers, farmers and produce vendors gathered under one roof to sell their wares to residents who lived within walking distance of the markets. These markets also became places to socialize and for public meetings. At one time, Cincinnati had as many as nine public markets in different areas of the city. But as the trolley and incline systems were constructed, people moved from the basin of the city to the hills. On each hill, neighborhood businesses, including grocery markets, popped up. The only remaining public market in Cincinnati today is the Findlay Market, near the Over-the-Rhine neighborhood.

In the late 1800s, Cincinnati was governed by a system of wards that lent themselves to corruption. From the 1880s until the 1920s, the Republican machine of Boss Cox primarily ran the city. By 1924, a new politician, Murray Seasongood, had instigated the ballot system to eliminate the corrupt wards.

The city was also the birthplace of two United States presidents. Benjamin Harrison, the twenty-third president, was elected in 1888 (at which time he resided in Indianapolis, Indiana). William Howard Taft was elected in 1909. The Tafts became a major political family in Ohio, with the president's son and grandson both becoming U.S. senators and his great-grandson, Bob Taft, being a two-term governor of the state.

People who came to America from different countries settled together in neighborhoods such as Over-the-Rhine for Germans and the West End for Eastern Europeans, especially Jews. In many neighborhoods, workshops, homes and businesses stood side by side. To accommodate the growing population, developers created "French flats," which, instead of being just sleeping rooms, were more traditional apartments that included private bathrooms and kitchens.

But the densely packed population in these areas created poor sanitation conditions that led to a cholera outbreak in 1867. To help ease these conditions, Cincinnati constructed suburban parks, new waterworks and broad avenues out of the city.

Despite the city's flaws, which were the same found in most urban areas at the time, to Louis Charles Graeter, Cincinnati was a haven.

A GRAETER MOVES TO CINCINNATI

Born in 1852, Louis Charles, son of immigrants from Germany, left his home in Madison, Indiana, as a teenager and moved to the Queen City. His grandchildren say they were told the young Graeter left home because his father, a barber, was "so mean to him," a quality they considered to be "typical" of their German heritage. Time would prove that the Graeters had a long history of being strong-willed, opinionated and not likely to shy from arguments.

Louis Charles landed in Cincinnati and began to sell ice cream at a street market at the base of Sycamore Hill. Making ice cream in those days was a painstaking—and expensive—process. Graeter made the treat by stirring it by hand in a metal pail set in a bucket filled with ice and salt, two expensive and hard-to-come-by items. The concoction had to be eaten almost immediately because there was no way to store it. Ice cream was, in those days, still considered a novel delicacy.

Graeter's Ice Cream was a newsworthy company in 1883, when the *Walnut Hills News* ran a blurb that stated: "Graeter's Ice Cream business is opening unusually good. He keeps two wagons engaged in delivering and three men employed in making his delicious creams."

But about the same time, Louis Charles decided that Cincinnati and the domestic life he had created with his wife, Anna, didn't suit him. He took $1,000 from his bank accounts and left his wife with the ice cream business and a fair amount of debt.

The Graeter family of Madison, Indiana. Young Louis Charles is on the far left. *Courtesy of Graeter's Ice Cream.*

Louis Charles set out to find his fortune in Stockton, California, where he married again. A different state and different faces offered only the same results for Louis Charles. Around the turn of the century, he left California and again returned to Cincinnati.

Louis Charles's brother, Fred, who had followed him to Cincinnati years earlier, was perhaps more noble than he. Fred had maintained the business and gotten it out of debt while Louis Charles was on the West Coast. When Louis Charles returned, Anna was gone, but the business was intact, so he resumed making ice cream in the French pots.

Maybe the hope for love knows no limits, or maybe the third time really is a charm, because Louis Charles again tried

Louis Charles Graeter, founder of Graeter's Ice Cream, was born in 1852 and moved to Cincinnati as a teenager. *Courtesy of Graeter's Ice Cream.*

his hand at marriage. He wed Regina Berger, who was the daughter of prominent Cincinnati businessman Anton Berger. Anton was an upstanding man in the community, president and general manager of the Julius J. Bantlin Company, which manufactured saddlery and hardware. Regina, his third child, was twenty-three years younger than her new husband. It appears that in Regina, Louis Charles had met his match.

The couple set up a home at 967 East McMillan Street in the Walnut Hills district of Cincinnati, a section at the top of the Main Street incline, one of the city's trolley systems. Louis Charles operated Graeter's Ice Cream out of their flat, cranking out the ice cream in the back room of the bottom floor and selling it out the front. Louis Charles and Regina lived in the upper floors. This store remained in operation until 1972. The property was sold in 1974.

Regina Berger (left) was the third wife of Louis Charles Graeter. She was twenty-three years his junior. *Courtesy of Graeter's Ice Cream.*

"There were a lot of companies like this in Cincinnati. They made it in the back room and sold it out the front door," said Lou Graeter, grandson and namesake to Louis Charles. "That's the way they ran the business. And they ran the business a long time that way."

To make the ice cream, Louis Charles still used what was called a French pot freezer, a handmade metal bowl that looked like a cylinder and sat inside a wooden bowl filled with ice and salt. Louis Charles filled the metal bowl with a mixture of cream, sugar and eggs.

"That pot would spin the mix and force the product to the sides and it would freeze," said Dick Graeter, another of Louis Charles's grandsons. "Then a person would stand there with a paddle and scrape that off the walls of that freezer until it all came together and was frozen." To spin the pots, Louis

Charles lined them up and hooked them by a pulley to a single motor overhead.

In addition to ice cream, which was primarily a summertime treat at that time, Graeter's sold chocolate confections and various knickknacks. Dick remembered:

> *At that time, we sold novelties, too. A lot of ceramics. In those days you didn't have all the gift stores and all these other places selling all that stuff. That was another thing that was an extra sale that you had in the wintertime when you weren't selling ice cream. All retail people are always looking for something else to sell, something that will pay the rent.*
>
> *Grandma always did that. She would go to New York a couple times a year and buy all this stuff and bring it back. And she'd send it to stores as part of the candy cases, different novelties, even toys and things.*

TRAGEDY AND TOUGH DECISIONS

Life was cut short for Louis Charles in 1919 at the age of sixty-seven, when a car struck him as he exited a trolley.

It was a scary time for Regina, who was left with two young sons, a business and not even the right to vote (which wasn't granted to women until the following year). The world was in the midst of its first world war and the largest flu epidemic in history. The war claimed an estimated sixteen million lives, while the flu that started in 1918 killed fifty million across the globe. A fifth of the world's population, and a quarter of the people in the United States, contracted the disease.

Cincinnati was changing during this period, too. A wartime shortage of labor and poor economic and social conditions in the southern states drove people north for factory jobs. Cincinnati became home to a large black population who settled primarily in the West End. While many were poor, black entrepreneurs settled in Cincinnati, too. Businesses such as a jazz bar called Cotton Club, which many say rivaled the club of the same name in New York, brought celebrities to the city and helped improve its image as an arts center in the Midwest. In later years, such notables as Ella Fitzgerald and Billie Holiday sang at the club.

The same year that Louis Charles was killed, the Cincinnati Reds won their first World Series against the Chicago White Sox. The title was soon tarnished, however, because members of the Chicago team were suspended for purposely losing the series for financial gain.

Graeter's was not the only family-owned ice cream business in town during this time. Thomas and Nicholas Aglamesis, who settled in Cincinnati from Sparta, Greece, started Aglamesis Brothers Ice Cream in 1908. The duo opened their first ice cream shop, called the Metropolitan, in Norwood, an eastern Cincinnati community. A second store in Oakley followed in 1913. The product was similar, though it was not made in French pots as Graeter's was. And, unlike the Graeters, the Aglamesis brothers were content with their two stores.

Regina had a different vision for her business. Despite being a young widow, she was determined to persevere, not just continuing with the single store but expanding it. She opened the first satellite stores on Walnut Street downtown and then in Hyde Park, which became one of Cincinnati's wealthiest enclaves. The store, which was originally part of Higginson's Tea Room, stood in Hyde Park Square, which was developed in 1900 as a center for shopping and community identity. This

The Graeter's store in Hyde Park is the oldest of the stores still in operation. It opened in 1920. *Courtesy of Ken Heigel.*

store at 2704 Erie Avenue is still in operation today and is the oldest operating Graeter's retail store.

To help with the family business, young Wilmer, the oldest son of Louis Charles and Regina, dropped out of school in the eighth grade, because he was more interested in driving a truck, his son Dick said.

"If Wilmer was around today, he would be one of those kids labeled ADHD," Dick said. "He was really smart, he just didn't do well in school." But he was, Dick remembers, very creative and artistic, an unusual combination of characteristics for someone who worked with his hands.

His younger brother, Paul, on the other hand, finished high school, though he didn't go to college.

By 1929, Regina had opened six new stores in Cincinnati, including ones in Norwood, Madisonville, Avondale and Pleasant Ridge. To manage the volume of ice cream needed, the company purchased a manufacturing facility on Reading Road in Mount Auburn in 1934 during the height of the Great Depression. The family turned a building that once housed an old printing press into an ice cream and chocolate production plant. All of the ice cream for the retail stores started being produced on Reading Road in 1937.

Graeter's
Fine Candies and Ice Cream

Tally

The back of a tally sheet from the 1930s lists store locations at the time. *Courtesy of The History Press.*

As history would prove over and over, people always made room for the little luxuries in life, such as ice cream. While other businesses faltered and failed, Graeter's grew during the most difficult economic time in the country's history.

By the end of World War II, Graeter's Ice Cream included a network of stores that spanned Cincinnati. By this time, Wilmer and Paul were heavily involved in the business, but it was Regina whom everyone, including her sons, called "the boss."

Her great-grandson, Richard Graeter II, believes she must have been a remarkable person, managing everything from the death of her husband to the business through two world wars and the Great Depression, at a time when most women didn't work outside the home at all, let alone run a business.

"I never met her, but I owe her for everything I have," her great-grandson Richard said, "because without her strength, fortitude and foresight, there would be no Graeter's Ice Cream today."

A CHANGING COUNTRY,
AN UNEASY ALLIANCE

By the 1940s, America was fully engaged in World War II on the European and Pacific fronts. While it took men from their homes to staff the military and forced rationing for the civilian public on everything from sugar to gasoline, the war alleviated unemployment. During the Great Depression, as many as eight million people were out of work, and another eight million lived below the poverty line. By 1941, the country had virtually no unemployment. In fact, some industries actually experienced labor shortages. Many women went to work, even in factories, to help with the war effort, making up 36 percent of the nation's total workforce by 1945.

As she had in the decades before, Regina Graeter remained at the helm of Graeter's Ice Cream through the war. The rationing of sugar became a particular problem because ice cream couldn't be made without it. "You couldn't get sugar," said Dick Graeter.

"I worked in a couple of stores during the war years. You'd almost run out of product. Eventually I think they started to get black market sugar, which helped considerably," he speculated.

The black market became a way of life for some people and businesses during the war because it was the only way they could get what they needed, whether that be meat, gasoline or sugar, albeit at a higher price.

One way that Americans helped in the war effort was to grow "victory gardens," in which they planted their own fruits and vegetables. It was estimated that by 1945, twenty million gardens produced 45 percent of America's produce.

After World War II, thousands of soldiers reentered the civilian workplace, and women returned to the home. Many businesses that had made money on the war now invested it in new plants and equipment for civilian production. Frugal Americans had saved money during the war that they now could spend on new houses and cars.

Marriage rates soared after the war, as did the birthrate, which became known as the Baby Boom. Between 1948 and 1953, more children were born than in the previous thirty years. In 1954, the country experienced the largest one-year population gain in history. The Baby Boom would reshape the American family for decades to come. In the late 1940s and early 1950s, for example, Americans considered it ideal to have a ranch or split-level house, one car and three children, with a husband and father as the primary breadwinner and a stay-at-home wife as mother and housekeeper. From this ideal sprang the suburbs: single-family homes with yards located away from industry. In Cincinnati, new subdivisions popped up in the surrounding hills of the city, and the new middle class flocked to them.

So many people left the downtown area that by the 1950s, Cincinnati underwent what was happening all over the country: urban renewal. But as happened in other cities, the renewal was done by bulldozer. Cincinnati embarked on the country's second largest slum clearance until that time. Thousands of buildings were razed, leaving thousands of families displaced.

The areas where Graeter's Ice Cream stores had originally expanded to—Oakley, the East End, Bond Hill—became increasingly working class and, in some cases, new slums. Stores set up by Regina had to move to follow the population that would buy ice cream, to places such as Westwood, Price Hill and Mariemont.

CHANGES IN ICE CREAM

It wasn't just the landscape of cities that changed. Advancements in manufacturing changed many things, from cars and appliances to ice cream.

Until after the war, virtually all ice cream manufacturers created their product by a method known as "batch freezing," which was similar to what was done at Graeter's, though not in true French pots. But after the war, commercial refrigeration and more sophisticated ice cream makers came along, and batch freezers disappeared. With the continuous commercial freezers, the mix of cream, sugar and eggs was poured in and quickly whipped with fast-moving beaters. These machines continuously spit out the ice cream—basically the antithesis of Graeter's.

At Graeter's, the mix was cranked in small batches—even today, a batch of Graeter's makes only two and a half gallons—and had to be scraped by hand from the sides of the pots and hand-packed into cartons. The Graeter's method incorporated the least amount of air into the ice cream, making it more dense and luxurious.

Dick Graeter remembers trying to make Graeter's Ice Cream in one of the newer ice cream makers when he joined the company in the 1950s. "You couldn't make the product that we were making in that type of a freezer. It would turn it into butter," Dick said. "I tried that several different times when I came here."

The new machines created a version of ice cream that was lighter in texture and airier than Graeter's. By law, ice cream could have as much as 100 percent overrun, or be as much as 50 percent whipped-in air. It was, in essence, frozen foam. Graeter's had (and still has) only a small amount of air that inevitably gets mixed in during the freezing process, just between 20 and 25 percent. A pint of Graeter's weighs almost a pound, whereas the competition's ice cream might weigh half as much.

Dick insists it wasn't just a pure love of the product that kept them from giving up the labor-intensive French pot method for a perhaps more lucrative continuous freezer version. "I always said that we were too dumb to make the next step, didn't know any better."

The changes in ice cream production came hand in hand with the onset of commercial dairy farms. The number of small dairy farms dwindled starting in the 1930s for more than fifty years because it became cost-prohibitive. Dairy farmers figured out what to feed cows to get the maximum output in milk. The annual average yield per cow rose from 3,000 pounds in 1890 to 4,500 pounds in 1950.

Insulated trucks led to larger milk-processing plants, which could process the milk at a much lower cost. Dairy products, including the milk and cream needed for ice cream, decreased in price. For dairy farms to make money, they needed bigger operations.

Local competition in ice cream increased with the introduction of United Dairy Farmers (UDF) in the 1940s. Started by Carl H. Lindner Sr. and carried on by his children, the group started one of the first dairy stores, where milk and

The plant at Reading Road includes pots for cream and men making the ice cream to the left. *Courtesy of the Cincinnati Historical Museum.*

other dairy products, including ice cream, were sold instead of home delivered. Despite growing popularity and convenience, the UDF ice cream was made by the continuous method, making the product a far cry from the hand-packed, dense ice cream made at Graeter's.

Another change to the ice cream industry was the introduction of soft serve, which became possible because of new equipment that hadn't been available until this time. "There was a soft serve place on every corner after the war," Dick said. "It really put the ice cream businesses like ours out of business. All ice cream like ours was sold in drugstores. There wasn't a drugstore anywhere that didn't have an ice cream fountain." Soft serve, sometimes referred to as frozen custard, was new and different—and widely available.

Like many culinary inventions, the history of soft serve is not definite. More than one claim to its creation exists. In one version, the silky smooth semi-frozen mixture was created by the founders of Dairy Queen, J.F. McCullough and his son, Alex, in Davenport, Illinois, about 1927. The duo decided to see if customers preferred ice cream in a softer state, before it was completely frozen. When they found that it was a hit with consumers, they started looking for machinery that would make it possible. In 1939, they found the necessary equipment. They opened the first Dairy Queen in 1940, and the phenomenon took off from there.

The competing story is that soft serve ice cream actually came from Thomas Carvelas, who was forced to sell partially frozen traditional ice cream on the streets in New York after he had a flat tire while delivering the fully frozen version. When customers loved it, he started making the softer version and selling it regularly. In this version of soft serve history, Carvelas actually invented the machine that creates the soft ice cream.

By 1956, soft serve ice cream consumption was increasing by 25 percent a year, according to the U.S. Department of Agriculture. And by that year, the three major chains—Dairy Queen, Carvel and Tastee-Freez—had more than two thousand locations across the country between them.

Another change Graeter's had to deal with was not in terms of competition but in advances in technology. The invention of the home freezer made it possible for customers to store ice cream at home. "In the '30s before the war most of the refrigerators had one little freezer compartment that wasn't separate. You really couldn't store ice cream. Any ice cream that you got you had to eat right away or you bought it out somewhere," Dick said. "When freezers were separated from the refrigerators, that really led to all the frozen food business. That did change the business significantly."

Attitudes after the war changed, too, Lou said. "Everybody stayed home and watched TV."

Staying home and being able to eat ice cream at home led to the production of ice cream novelties such as the Cho Cho Bar, basically chocolate ice cream on a stick, which was sold for a nickel.

WILMER'S WAYS

As for their own childhood, Dick, Lou and Kathy Graeter, Wilmer's oldest daughter, say they don't remember actually eating that much ice cream. "I don't think we did eat much ice cream when we were kids because I don't think he brought it home," Dick said of his father. "Ice cream was more of a treat in those days."

But Dick and Lou both remember their father being able to eat a large quantity of ice cream.

What Kathy remembers most about her father is his work ethic. "He was always a very hard worker. He enjoyed what he was doing all the time," she said. "He had a real appreciation for what the product is: unique, something special."

It was also Wilmer, Dick and Lou believe, who came up with the idea of adding chocolate chips to the ice cream. Those chips and the way they are added are one of the hallmarks of the Graeter's Ice Cream enjoyed today.

"Howard Johnson made the first chocolate chip ice cream. And everybody kind of copied from them," Dick said. But the way Graeter's adds chocolate chips to its ice cream is unique and hasn't changed since they started doing it: melted chocolate mixed with a small amount of vegetable oil is added to the spinning pot of cream, sugar and eggs when the ice cream is almost completely frozen. (The vegetable oil guarantees the chocolate will melt in the mouth at the same temperature as the ice cream, Dick says.) It spins for a few minutes to harden into a shell and then is scraped off by hand with a paddle into the ice cream, resulting in different size chunks. It is a process that can't be duplicated by the big continuous freezers, Dick says. "They have a fruit feeder that adds the chips at some point when the ice cream is partially frozen. But they can't do it the same way we do it," he said. "Ours comes out with actual pieces of chocolate of different sizes. You can't do that with commercial equipment. That's one of the unique things we do that no one else can do."

Originally, the only flavors Graeter's offered were vanilla and chocolate scooped into a dish or a cone. But Wilmer also had a knack for making molded ice cream. He would pack the ice cream into pretty molds in all sorts of shapes, like flowers and fruits. He would freeze them, unmold them and decorate them using a little hand pump spray atomizer.

"He had quite an artistic flair for them," Lou said. "We made them to order for Sunday brunches and parties. My dad would pack them on ice and rock salt and hand deliver them." World War II brought an end to the molded ice cream, and the company never brought it back.

Another treat that has been part of the Graeter family for decades, but never sold, is what they call "lollipops." To make them, balls of vanilla ice cream are hand-dipped into the same chocolate used to make the chocolate chips, completely enclosing the ice cream. They're served frozen on a stick. Richard says he remembers Dick and Lou making them for family gatherings, but now the responsibility falls to Lou's youngest son, Chip.

Wilmer was responsible for ice cream sundaes at Graeter's, too, creating what he called bittersweet topping sometime before World War II. The ice cream sundae had been invented sometime in the late 1800s, though, like ice cream itself, the actual creation stories vary. One popular story suggests that it was created and named so ice cream shops could be open on Sunday, the Christian Sabbath. Another version says it was an accident of spilled syrup on ice cream that became so popular that store owners feared they would lose money on it. So they made it a Sunday-only special, giving it its name.

Where Graeter's differed from other ice cream shops of the time was in the chocolate topping it used for the sundaes. All the other ice cream shops simply used chocolate syrup. "My father made the first fudge topping. We call it bittersweet but it's actually fudge. He made that from the Hershey cocoa," Dick said. "There're two kinds of cocoas you normally have. One is Dutch process, which is processed with an alkali. The other is natural process. The natural process cocoa will get thick when you cook it, whereas the Dutch process, no matter what you do, will not get thick. What he did, what we still do, is use the natural process cocoa to make our bittersweet topping."

Before the war, Wilmer tried to strike a deal with Hershey's to create a chocolate specifically for Graeter's bittersweet topping. "But the war came along and Hershey didn't want anything to do with us," Lou remembers. "We were too little to mess with," Dick said.

Another problem, however, was that chocolate became hard to come by once the war started. It was turned into K rations and sent overseas for soldiers. Chocolate was valued because it was high in calories, and K rations were created to make sure the troops ingested enough calories to sustain them in battle. The chocolate was vitamin-fortified and modified so it wouldn't melt in the heat.

Today, the company uses what it considers a better chocolate for its topping as well as the chips in the ice cream. Both come from a spinoff of Nestle called Mr. Peter's. It's also the chocolate used to make Graeter's candy.

About the same time as sundaes, parfaits became popular at soda fountains and were added to the menu at Graeter's, too.

They were sold in tall glasses as layers of ice cream and sauce topped with whipped cream. The main difference between parfaits and sundaes, according to historians, is the dish in which each is served. Sundaes were served simply in shallow bowls, while parfaits were concocted in tall, thin, tulip-shaped glasses. "Think of it as your fanciest sundae," said Richard.

Menus from the '30s show that parfaits sold for thirty cents, while a bowl of ice cream sold for fifteen cents and a sundae sold for twenty cents.

Milkshakes, too, have been part of the Graeter's stores for as long as anyone can remember. Historically, milkshakes and malteds were initially considered health foods. Malted milk was created as an easily digested wheat and malted barley product for infants and invalids. Drugstore soda fountains soon realized they could add the malted powders to ice cream and blend it into a wholesome drink. Milkshakes became particularly popular in the 1920s with the invention of the electric blender.

Richard believes in those days milkshakes were made to be thin, "Something that could be sucked down in ten seconds flat." Milkshakes today, in Richard's opinion, even those sold at Graeter's, are much too thick. "A milkshake should have just one scoop of ice cream, the rest milk and chocolate syrup," he said.

In addition to the basic ice cream flavors, Graeter's would, on occasion, offer seasonal flavors, including strawberry and peach, when the fruits were in season. Dick and Lou remember these seasonal flavors, though not necessarily with fondness because of the work entailed for them. "That was our summer job. We always peeled peaches, put them up in wooden barrels and put them in cold storage," Dick said.

Eventually, the company was able to prep enough peaches to keep in cold storage so it could make the flavor all year. Strawberries, however, were strictly seasonal. "In

Graeter's Ice Creams

Still made the Old Fashioned Way

HAND PACKED..2.60 Pint
CHIP FLAVORS 2.80
BITTER-
SWEET ......1.65 ½ Pt.
OTHER
SYRUPS ....1.35 ½ Pt.
DISH 1.10
CHIP FLAVORS 1.20
CONES ....70¢, 1.30, 1.90
CHIP FLAVORS
75¢, 1.40, 2.00

Vanilla/with the Bean
Chocolate
Pistachio
Peach
Strawberry
Black Walnut
Macaroon
Caramel
Butter Pecan
Black Cherry
Peppermint Stick
Coffee
Chocolate Chip
Double Chocolate Chip
Chocolate Mint Chip
Chocolate Mocha Chip
Black Raspberry
Coconut

Fresh Fruit Ices

HAND PACKED..2.05 Pint
Lemon
Orange
Pineapple
Raspberry
Lime
Strawberry

Pleasing Parfaits* 1.75

Served with Whipped Cream, Nuts and Cherry

Chocolate	Strawberry
Marshmallow	Pineapple
Chocolate Marshmallow	Wild Cherry
Butterscotch	Raspberry
Nectar	Cherry Fruit

Hot Fudge or Bittersweet 1.80

Sundaes* 1.35

Featuring GRAETER'S Homemade Syrups

Chocolate	Strawberry
Cherry Fruit	Wild Cherry
Chocolate Marshmallow	Pineapple
Marshmallow	Raspberry
Butterscotch	Vanilla
Nectar	

Hot Fudge or Bittersweet 1.45

Scrumptious Sundaes* 1.75

Served with Whipped Cream, Crispy Pecans and Cherry
Hot Fudge or Bittersweet 1.85

Extras

Whipped Cream 25¢, Chopped Nuts 25¢,
Two Syrups, 25¢
Chocolate Sprills, 20¢

Specials*

Swiss Chocolate 1.70	Persian Nut 1.85	
Banana Special 2.35	2 Dip Dish,	
The "Whole Banana"	2 Flavors 1.40	
White Tower 1.55	Turtle Sundae 1.85	
WEBN 1.45	Child's Dish	
	(under 6) .... .80	

All Fountain Items available to take out
*Parfaits, Sundaes & Sodas & Specials with Chip Flavors 10¢ Extra

Double Dip Sodas* 1.65

Chocolate
Strawberry
Pineapple
Cherry Fruit
Wild Cherry
Vanilla
Chocolate Mint
Lemon
Lime
Nectar
Raspberry
Root Beer

Drinks

Milk Shake 1.20
(Extra Scoop 45¢)
Malted Milk 1.25
(Extra Scoop 45¢)
Lemonade ....75¢
(Plain)
Lemonade 1.25
(With Lemon Ice)
Freezes 1.15
Pepsi-Cola ....65¢
Diet Pepsi ....65¢
Flavored Pepsi ......75¢
Root Beer ....65¢
Phosphates ....65¢

The inside of the menu lists the ice cream flavors, sundaes and other specialties. *Courtesy of the Cincinnati Historical Museum.*

Two men making ice cream in the French pots at the Reading Road plant. *Courtesy of the Cincinnati Historical Museum.*

those days, they didn't have any prepared strawberries like frozen strawberries. We only made strawberry during the strawberry season," Dick said. "And that was a nasty job. That was labor intensive. Our dad brought us to work pretty young, pretty early."

Lou also remembers the hard work from a young age. "We were squeezing lemons, peeling peaches. As soon as we got strong enough we were on those French pots," he said.

SIBLING CONFLICTS

Regina, whom everyone called "the boss," worked with her sons to run Graeter's Ice Cream. But it was no secret that brothers Wilmer and Paul shared an animosity toward one another. "They didn't get along when they were kids," Lou said. "They never got away from that."

Regina arranged the business so they both did what they were best at: Wilmer made the ice cream at the plant, while Paul handled the stores and the banking. "Grandma kind of set it up to keep them together," said Dick.

The problem was the brothers didn't appreciate what the other did. Wilmer was in charge of production of ice cream at the plant with his mother, while Paul managed the stores. Lou remembers his father grumbling that Paul was never at the plant.

"Paul would go around to the stores in the morning. Then he'd come in around noontime and spend about two hours," he said. "But then he would just leave."

But Paul did bring positive components to Graeter's, including adding the bakery business that was built up significantly through the '60s and '70s. The bakery is still part of the company today.

Wilmer Graeter (left) with his oldest son, Lou, who also worked in the family business. *Courtesy of Graeter's Ice Cream.*

"We were just going to make desserts. Pies, cakes," Lou remembers. But they quickly realized that wasn't enough. "They found out they couldn't be in the bakery business unless they started making a little bit of everything. Everything from pies and cakes to rolls and Danish and coffee cakes. I mean the full line of retail baked products," Dick said.

Today, the company offers that full line of fresh-baked goods, from coffee cakes—including the famous double butter cake along with pecan and plain tea rings—to a range of donuts and Danish rolls, as well as butter-crusted bread, butterbit dinner rolls and, in the summer season, hot dog and hamburger buns. In addition, the company makes decorated cakes, cupcakes, éclairs, cookies, cream horns and turnovers.

One other aspect of the bakery business draws cakes and ice creams together into what was considered a

In Cincinnati, Graeter's also sells its own line of baked goods as well as chocolates. *Courtesy of Ken Heigel.*

fanciful dessert of the eighteenth century: ice cream cakes, or bombes. Cakes are layered with ice cream and topped with whipped cream and sometimes a chocolate glaze. In addition, Graeter's also makes "wheelies," or novelties that sandwich ice cream between two cookies. It's a variation of a dessert that gained popularity at the turn of the century in San Francisco called an It's It bar, which was made with oatmeal cookies. At Graeter's, the wheelies are made with chocolate chip cookies.

After Regina died in 1955 at the age of eighty, her sons tried to work together, but it was an uneasy alliance. Eventually, Wilmer bought Paul out.

"It was either they split up or they probably would have gone out of business," Dick said.

Wilmer's grandson, Richard, thinks Paul knew it was better for him to go than Wilmer. "He was more sophisticated than

Grandpa," he said. "He had done well with money, had enough to live on."

For Wilmer, Richard said, Graeter's Ice Cream was his life. But the buyout took a certain toll on the family, too. "There was a complete split in our family. When he [Paul] left, it's like he fell off the earth. We never saw him again," Dick said. It was a lesson Dick and the rest of the family would have to face again, when it was their turn to transition between generations.

When Regina died, the company went through other changes as well. It got out of the novelty business, concentrating instead on ice cream, chocolates and baked goods. Wilmer and his children also decided it was time to reinvest in the company to grow and preserve it for future generations.

THIRD GENERATION

If the '50s were a time of home and family, the '60s were a time of great upheaval in America.

The decade introduced the era of the civil rights movement, which led to a time of distinct civil unrest. By 1960, half of the black population had moved from the southern states to urban areas in the North, where many lived in poverty. While many followed the nonviolence preached by Martin Luther King Jr., others found identity in more radical groups that encouraged revolution, such as the Black Panthers.

Cincinnati was not immune to the civil rights struggle. Many blacks in Cincinnati who were displaced by the urban renewal of the '50s, as well as the ones who moved up from the southern states, settled in the Over-the-Rhine area or the West End. The influx gave the neighborhood the highest population density in Cincinnati—as well as the second-lowest income level of anywhere in the city. New slums were created when landlords subdivided larger houses into smaller apartments. High crime followed. City government tried to improve the conditions by creating a social services center and concentrating renewal funds on the areas' redevelopment.

But change was slow to come, and the city felt the backlash. Riots that left two people dead broke out in Cincinnati after the shooting death of King in Memphis in 1968.

The '60s were also the time of the women's rights movement. Women fought hard for equal rights, tossing to the wind the notion that true fulfillment came solely from caring for a husband and children. Betty Friedan's *The Feminine Mystique* and the formation of the National Organization for Women (NOW) championed to pass the Equal Rights Amendment to the Constitution that would have made gender discrimination illegal. The amendment never passed, but greater access to birth control gave women more control over their bodies and, ultimately, their lives.

With women seeking new roles in the world, the concept of marriage changed. Many couples decided to marry later and held off on having children. With the '60s also came a higher rate of divorce.

For Cincinnati, the '60s brought some positive changes, including a new National Football League franchise. In 1967, owner Paul Brown formed the Cincinnati Bengals, named for the Bengal tigers housed at the nationally renowned Cincinnati Zoo & Botanical Garden.

With both a professional baseball and a football team, Cincinnati needed a stadium to support them and their fans. With the help of Ohio governor James A. Rhodes, the city agreed to build a multipurpose stadium on the dilapidated riverfront section of the city. The facility, named Riverfront Stadium, opened in 1970 and was built in the same style as Atlanta–Fulton County Stadium, St. Louis's Busch Stadium and Pittsburgh's Three River Stadium. Riverfront, however, was the first stadium in which the playing surface was covered in Astroturf, or artificial grass.

Riverfront, which could hold almost fifty-three thousand people, was also home to the Cincinnati Reds, who became a powerhouse in Major League Baseball in the '70s. The team won back-to-back World Series in 1975 and '76 with players including Pete Rose, Joe Morgan, George Foster and Johnny Bench. During this era, the Reds became known as "the Big Red Machine."

New Graeters in an Old Business

The third generation of Graeters came into the business in the midst of these changes in the late 1950s and into the '60s, working closely with their father, Wilmer, after he bought out his brother, Paul. The three boys, Lou, Dick and Jon, were all born within two years of one another.

Lou, the oldest, joined Graeter's Ice Cream full time after a couple of years at Ohio State University and four years in the navy. "I got a draft notice, but I didn't want to go in the army," Lou said. "I wanted to go in the navy." He waited until he could enlist in the navy, but then he had to serve four years instead of the two required with the draft notice. "It was just as well. I was no good in school anyway," Lou said. "The day after I got home I came right here."

Dick graduated from Ohio State and also spent a couple of years in the army. Unlike his siblings, he tried his hand outside the family business. "I actually worked for Gibson Greeting Cards for a couple of years when I got out of the service," he said. "It was like a management training program there."

The primary reason he didn't go into the family business, he said, was that everyone else was already in the business. His father and uncle Paul were still partners, and his grandmother was still alive and actively working. Lou went into the business

Kathy, Dick and Lou Graeter are three of the five grandchildren of Louis Charles and Regina Graeter. *Courtesy of the Graeter family.*

right after the service, not leaving a lot of room for anyone else. "It was already a family business with too much family in it. So somebody had to not be in it," Dick said. He became part of Graeter's Ice Cream a few years after his grandmother, Regina, died in 1955, about the same time his oldest daughter, Cindy, was born.

Like his brothers, Jon came into the business after college, handling the company's finances.

Kathy, the only girl in the family business, worked in the stores or at the plant in the summers between school. She was an avid and accomplished tennis player, winning eight singles titles at the Metropolitan tennis tournament in Cincinnati and an international mixed doubles tournament in Monaco. But she says she never gave any thought to joining the professional circuit. In fact, she said she never had any thoughts of doing anything but working in the family business. After graduating

The original Graeter's store on McMillan still shows the hand-lettered sign, even though the building itself is now dilapidated. *Courtesy of Ken Heigel.*

from Northwestern University, she joined the Graeter's team and was put in charge of the retail stores in 1962. She did, however, continue to play competitive tennis, remaining a number-one seed at area tournaments through two more decades.

For her professional life, Kathy said that working with her dad and her brothers was a good experience. "We always respected each other. It's just kind of in your blood." Nonetheless, Kathy was not made an owner until decades later, when Jon retired and she was able to buy out his shares.

One other sister, Carol, never became part of the business, though she, too, worked summers at the retail stores.

Dividing up who managed which aspects of the business happened naturally, the siblings say. "I wound up kind of in charge of the bakery. Lou did the candy. Father did the ice cream," Dick said. "They made me do a little bit of everything. I kind of gravitated toward the bakery a little bit because there really was nobody doing that. And it was a pretty crude operation."

The family spent much of the '60s and '70s reinvesting in the company, something that hadn't been done in the decade before. In 1972, they finally closed the original store on McMillan Street because the neighborhood had become so poor. They sold the property in 1974.

OODLES OF COMPETITION

The decades managed by the third generation of Graeters came filled with challenges but with some unexpected help, too. The ice cream business was steady but slow in the '60s, but then it started to pick up.

"I think what changed, what helped our business as much as anything, was people like Baskin-Robbins when they moved in the Midwest," Dick said. "I think that did as much for our ice cream as anything. Because it got people interested and thinking about ice cream cones, sundaes and that type of thing more than they had before. Before that people started eating ice cream at home."

During the '60s, most people would only go out occasionally for ice cream cones. However, they would stop by Graeter's to buy pints of ice cream to take home on a more regular basis. "That business grew significantly through the '60s and '70s," Dick said.

But when Baskin-Robbins came along, the ice cream landscape changed. Baskin-Robbins was started in Pasadena, California, by brothers-in-law Burt Baskin and Irv Robbins in the 1940s. The stores became franchise only because Baskin and Robbins felt that on-site managers with a financial stake in the company would maintain the quality better. The stores focused on "fun" flavors such as bubble gum and pralines 'n' cream. By the mid-'60s, the company had more than four hundred stores nationally. In Cincinnati, Baskin-Robbins tried to open stores in the same neighborhoods as Graeter's but met with little success.

"It cost you the same for an ice cream cone at Baskin-Robbins as it did at Graeter's," Dick said. "But it was an obvious difference in the quality between ours and theirs. They didn't [succeed] because people could compare one with the other, and ours wasn't really significantly more expensive, but it was significantly better. All ice cream is good. Ours, I like to say, is unique. People like the uniqueness in a product."

A story by the *Cincinnati Enquirer* in 1979 led the way for the rivalries between the upcoming national brands versus local favorites. In an unofficial taste test with children as judges, Graeter's outscored Baskin-Robbins in the strawberry flavor (the other longtime Cincinnati ice cream maker, Aglamesis

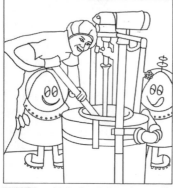

GRAETER'S ICE CREAM SINCE 1870 It is time for us to discover ice cream. The computer read out advises going to Graeter's . . . Beep. But, why Graeter's? . . . Beep. Graeter's is the last ice cream company to make ice cream by hand. And is it good! . . . Beep.

HYDE PARK GRAETER'S This is the Hyde Park Graeter's. Let's try a cone with two dips of ice cream . . . Beep. That's tradition and good taste all in one . . . Beep.

Above: Coloring pages such as these with an alien/robot theme were often given out to kids who visited Graeter's. *Courtesy of the Cincinnati Historical Museum.*

Left: Inside, the Hyde Park store still feels like it did ninety years ago when it opened. *Courtesy of Ken Heigel.*

Brothers, took first place). Outsiders Baskin-Robbins came in first in the chocolate tasting, outscoring Graeter's and the Aglamesis Brothers. Häagen-Dazs, the other national brand in the taste test, never scored better than Graeter's.

The tasting was not a sign of strong competition for Graeter's, however. Today, there are only three Baskin-Robbins locations in Cincinnati, while there are fourteen Graeter's Ice Cream stores.

Along with fun, Baskin-Robbins competition proved to be good for Graeter's on another level. The advent of "super-premium" ice cream brought national players with deep pockets, including Häagen-Dazs and Ben & Jerry's, into the market.

Before the late '70s and early '80s, the ice cream market could be basically divided into two categories: premium ice cream and value ice cream. The main difference was in the quality of ingredients and the amount of butterfat and overrun, or air pumped into the ice cream during the processing. The more air, the less dense the finished product. Super-premium ice cream introduced the country to a whole new version of the sweet treat—or so some of the makers wanted the public to believe. In actuality, Graeter's had been making a super-premium ice cream all along.

Häagen-Dazs came out of a company called Senator's Ice Cream in New York that had spent years in the first part of the 1900s making cheap ice cream with high overrun and low butterfat. Its high-end entry started in the late '50s by switching the old formula on its head, with a low overrun and high butterfat, a similar product to what Graeter's had always made.

Super-premium ice cream was also significantly more expensive than other value and premium brands on the market, which made its popularity seem counterintuitive. The '80s brought a humbling recession, an unemployment rate of a historically high 7.5 percent and inflation at more than

The Graeter Tradition!

Graeter's is . . . lots of cream, fresh daily . . . farm fresh eggs . . . vanilla beans from Madagascar and Mexico ground for true flavor . . . our own blend of cocoas, domestic and imported, for a matchless chocolate taste . . . peaches especially 'put up' in summer so fresh peach ice cream can be enjoyed all year 'round . . . fruit ices made from fresh natural juices . . . toppings . . . old family recipes . . . swiss chocolate prepared at each store . . . distinctive bittersweet and nectar, plus your all time favorites . . . that extra touch of whipped cream made fresh daily . . . ice cream still hand made . . . the unique french pot way . . . a taste that's old fashioned and wholesome . . . a taste found only at Graeter's.

We are equally proud of our other fine products . . . a variety of select candies . . . a complete line of delectable pastries baked daily in our kitchens . . . take some home and enjoy them today.

STORES

41 East Fourth Street, Downtown
332 Ludlow Ave., Clifton
2704 Erie Ave., Hyde Park
Kenwood Mall Shopping Center
6918 Wooster Pike, Mariemont
2376 Ferguson Rd.
5923 Hamilton Ave., College Hill
11511 Princeton Rd.
6100 Glenway Ave., Western Hills Plaza
895 W. Galbraith, Finneytown
Plant and Office — 2145 Reading Rd.

On a menu from Graeter's probably from the '60s or '70s, the business tradition is explained. *Courtesy of the Cincinnati Historical Museum.*

13 percent. But at the same time, consumers wanted higher-quality products and were willing to pay for them. The mentality seemed to be that maybe consumers couldn't buy a new house or car, but if they were going to buy ice cream, it was going to be the good stuff, not sweet, artificially flavored frozen air.

Despite the health concerns that cropped up later in the decade, ice cream—especially super-premium ice cream—became an affordable indulgence. In *Ben & Jerry's: The Inside Scoop*, author Fred "Chico" Lager wrote, "Weight Watchers had studies that showed that ice cream was the number one food people gave up their diets for. It was America's favorite dessert, and people seemed more inclined to make an exception for ice cream than anything else."

With its faux Danish name (Häagen-Dazs does not translate into anything in Danish or any other language; owner Reuben Mattus made it up) and high-quality product, Häagen-Dazs created a newfound appreciation for ice cream. By the '80s, all the major manufacturers had come out with super-premium lines of ice cream with foreign-sounding names, such as Frusen Gladje, Le Glace de Paris and Alphen Zauber.

Ben & Jerry's was a similar high-quality product with humble roots, this time in Vermont in the late '70s. What made Ben & Jerry's different was its social conscience. The company used local products to support farmers and gave money to help fund charities, such as a drug counseling center and homeless shelter in Harlem. It also set up a nonprofit arm called Ben & Jerry's Foundation, to which a portion of the company's profits were granted. The foundation then donated the money in the form of grants to other nonprofit organizations.

Unlike elegant, super smooth Häagen-Dazs, Ben & Jerry's turned to super-chunky fun flavors such as New York Super Fudge Chunk, Dastardly Mash—a combination of pecans, walnuts, chocolate chips and raisins in a chocolate ice cream base—and Cherry Garcia with cherries and chocolate.

And while Häagen-Dazs was slick, Ben & Jerry's was homespun. In those days, co-founder Ben Cohen was known to say, "We're the only super-premium ice cream whose name you can pronounce."

Both companies rolled out a limited number of scoop shops across the country but also made their ice cream available by the pint at some grocery stores. (Both companies have since been purchased by large corporations: Häagen-Dazs by Pillsbury, which was eventually acquired by Nestle, and Ben & Jerry's by Unilever.)

To compete with these new super-premium ice creams, Graeter's turned to grocery stores. The company had sold its products to an exclusive market called Washington Market in the TriBeCa neighborhood of New York in the early '80s but was surprised to discover that the store was in turn selling the pints for a whopping $8.85 (in Cincinnati, at the time, a pint went for $2.50).

So in 1987, Graeter's decided to stay closer to home and struck a deal with Kroger, the largest grocery chain in the Midwest, to start selling Graeter's pints. By 1990, eleven Kroger stores also had soda fountains so customers could get a scoop of ice cream while they shopped and could then pick up a pint to take home.

But one newcomer of the '80s proved decidedly difficult for ice cream producers, including Graeter's: frozen yogurt. During the '80s—and ever since— consumers became concerned with sugar and fat, two things ice cream couldn't be made well without. About the same time, a new product, frozen yogurt, came onto the market.

Frozen yogurt is made much like ice cream but with milk and water instead of cream and eggs and with the addition of yogurt culture. When frozen yogurt was first introduced in

The front of a coupon from 1989 offers a free scoop of ice cream from Graeter's stores. *Courtesy of the Cincinnati Historical Museum.*

the '70s, it was a dismal failure because consumers thought it tasted too much like regular yogurt. Manufacturers reformulated the product into something sweeter and more like soft serve ice cream, but still with a "healthy halo." A half cup of TCBY frozen yogurt, one of the most popular shops that popped up during the era, contained roughly half the calories, less sugar and just a fraction of the fat of a half-cup portion of Graeter's Ice Cream. Later, some frozen yogurt took on more of a traditional hard-frozen ice cream appearance, and makers including Häagen-Dazs got in on the action.

Dick said sales in the '80s leveled off specifically because of the introduction of frozen yogurt. But he didn't worry; he considered the treat to be a flash in the pan.

"Frozen yogurt is the fad food of 1988," said Dick in an article in the *Cincinnati Enquirer* in 1988. "It's a fad that will grow and will peak, and then it will start dropping off. We'll wait until the fad passes."

Dick was right about it being a fad. By the '90s, soft serve frozen yogurt had all but disappeared, though new versions such as Pinkberry and Red Mango have started making another run on the ice cream market in the latter part of the first decade of the 2000s. And refrigerator cases at supermarkets still contain a brand or two of hard frozen yogurt, including Häagen-Dazs and UDF.

A "NEW" FRENCH POT—AND FRANCHISEES

If the steady competition wasn't challenging enough, during the same time it became clear that the company would have to begin replacing some of its aging French pots. Graeter's was still using the same cypress wood vats, old tin bowls and maplewood paddles for scraping the ice cream from the sides of the pots. "We basically made ice cream on one-hundred-year-old antique ice cream machines," Richard said.

The family needed something new and more reliable that wouldn't compromise the high-end, handmade quality of their ice cream. It proved difficult to find a suitable replacement.

For a time, they turned to Alvey Washing Equipment Company in Cincinnati to make stainless steel vats to replace the cypress bowls. They switched from the maplewood paddles to a plastic composite. But the new version of the actual machine was harder to replace.

When Dick attended a bakery trade show in 1978, he saw an ice cream maker made by an Italian company called Carpigiani that was similar to the French pot. Instead of a hand-operated paddle, it had a corkscrew scraper that turned automatically. The company bought one machine to see how it would work.

The results were good enough that Graeter's could achieve one of its long-term goals: making the ice cream in-store instead of just at the plant. The first place Graeter's tried this was at the Colerain Avenue store.

But ultimately, the Carpigiani machine didn't work for Graeter's. "We finally decided they weren't heavy-duty enough for what we were doing with it," Dick said. The machine was designed to make gelato, a slightly softer version of ice cream than what Graeter's produced.

But it did give them an idea of what they needed in a new French pot, and the company set to work at designing its own machine. "We probably reinvented that machine a couple of times," Dick said. "I know we had to spend a million dollars over time, maybe more."

Graeter's Ice Cream now manufactures the machines it uses for production today, still using the basic principle of the French pot. It doesn't have a patent on the actual machine, though it considers the company that makes it to be proprietary information. Still, Dick said he doesn't worry about anyone stealing the concept. "Nobody really wants to make product this way."

In the end, it's the production that sets ice cream apart, according to Dick. All ice cream recipes, he says, are basically the same. "There's no real secret recipe to ice cream. There's cream, sugar and eggs," Dick said. "I don't care whether it's Häagen-Dazs or Ben & Jerry's or Graeter's. It's still cream, sugar and eggs."

Expanding by Franchising

With a number of retail stores running successfully, the Graeters decided to try expanding their business by franchising in the '80s.

In 1985, Graeter's Ice Cream offered a license store to Lyle Brumfield. He was permitted to open one, at most two, stores in Kentucky, a new area for the company. When the arrangement worked well, the Graeters became more comfortable with the idea of a true franchise.

In 1989, Graeter's entered into a franchise deal with Maury Levine and Clay Cookery of Columbus. But it had taken the duo years and an inside connection to get the deal in place, though it had been their dream since just after college. "After business school, I went to work for P&G [Procter & Gamble]," Levine remembers. One of the first places new friends took him was to Graeter's Ice Cream. "As soon as you taste it, you can instantly tell it's better than anything else you've ever had. It's a marketer's dream."

Levine married Susan Sachs, who had roomed with Dick's daughter Cindy at Miami University. Through his wife, Levine and Cookery met Dick and became social friends. After eight years, Graeter's finally sold them the franchise. "I think they had an interest in expanding, but they never had the ability because they were very hands-on," Levine said. Richard says it was the persistence of the duo—and their apparent business savvy—that finally convinced Dick to sell them a franchise.

Levine and Cookery opened the first Columbus store on Lane Avenue on August 24, 1989. The franchise agreement allowed them to make the ice cream according to the recipes and specifications of Graeter's and on the leased French pot machines. They were allowed to open stores within Franklin and, eventually, Montgomery Counties.

Levine and Cookery expanded to eleven stores in Columbus and four more in Dayton, but never without careful planning. Levine, who said it was a joy working for Dick, remembers Dick's words of wisdom when it came to opening stores: "Once you're dead, you're dead a long time."

Since 2000, all of the Graeter's Ice Cream sold in Columbus and Dayton—including that sold at grocery stores—has been made at the Bethel Road location, where the plant portion of the store is glass-enclosed and customers can watch the ice cream being made.

After offering a franchise to Levine and Cookery, Graeter's changed the license agreement with Brumfield in Kentucky to be a full franchise so that he could open stores anywhere in the state. Jim Tedesko, a homegrown Cincinnatian, was a certified public accountant at the time, and Brumfield was one of his clients. Brumfield convinced him to come to work for him in the franchise operation in Kentucky in 1997. Not long after, Tedesko decided he wanted his own franchise, so he approached the Graeters about expanding to Indianapolis.

"They said they weren't set up for Indiana and suggested I buy the Louisville portion from Brumfield," Tedesko said. So in 1998, that's what he did.

For Tedesko, being a franchise owner of Graeter's was ideal. "I was born and raised in Cincinnati, so I grew up on the product," he said. "I wanted to be in business for myself. And over the years I'd become familiar with their processes."

Now Tedesko is the owner of eight stores in Louisville and the ten surrounding counties. In addition he owns a ten-thousand-square-foot plant, where he produces the ice cream for all of the Louisville stores and, as in Columbus, for all the Louisville grocery stores that carry it, too.

"It's such a labor-intensive product, we have to make it locally," Tedesko said. "Customers, the press talk about

Graeter's being a Cincinnati-based company, but the ice cream we sell is really homemade in Louisville."

Brumfield eventually retired and sold the northern Kentucky part of his business in 2003 to Zaki Barakat, who now owns four Graeter's stores.

"The original concept of the franchise was that they would have a couple of these machines and operate them on premises, manufacturing, selling," Dick said. "But most of them, like Columbus, started at one store and made it in the back room then used that store as the manufacturing then opened up the satellite stores."

SPECIAL FLAVORS

The basic ingredients may be the same, but there are some Graeter's flavors no one else has been able to duplicate. Black raspberry ice cream, for example, was Dick's creation. "I was the first one to make black raspberry. The reason I made it: I could find the puree to make it with," he said.

The flavor was a childhood memory for him. "I remember as a youngster buying black raspberry ice cream from the local drugstore. All the soda fountains at the drugstores had black raspberry," he said. "For some reason I liked it."

Later—Dick doesn't remember the exact date, though he thinks it was in the 1970s—he tried adding chocolate chips to the black raspberry flavor. It quickly became—and remains—the bestselling Graeter's flavor, accounting for 20 percent of total sales of the ice cream.

Dick said they made the black raspberry both with and without chips for a long time but eventually got rid of the one without chips, much to his dismay, because it didn't sell as well. "I quit eating black raspberry when I put the chips in. I don't like it. I never liked it."

Lou, however, is a big fan of the chocolate chip flavors, including black raspberry chocolate chip, though his favorite flavor is mocha chocolate chip. For customers, too, the flavors with chocolate chips are by far the favorite, accounting for 70 percent of total ice cream sales.

For Kathy, her favorite flavor remains the simplest: vanilla. "I like the texture of the smoothness, the coolness," she said. And while she doesn't mind the chocolate chips in some flavors, she says, "I always want my final bite to be vanilla." She feels the customers enjoy the chocolate chip flavors so much because it's an indulgence. To the Graeter family, who eat ice cream every day, it's a little too much.

Another of Dick's contributions is the rotating seasonal flavors. He came up with the concept, he says, to keep customers coming back. "I just did one a month. We'd run it for six or seven weeks then drop it," he said. "You can almost tell by the month what flavor I had."

Coconut was in January, followed by cherry chocolate chip in February and chocolate almond in March. July always brought peach, and the fall brought autumn flavors such as pumpkin in October, cinnamon in November and peppermint and eggnog in December. Now the company offers seasonal flavors instead of monthly flavors, bringing in a few different ones for longer stretches: peach, for example, might run from July to August, and strawberry chocolate chip, a spring favorite, will begin in April and run through May.

SHIPPING TO NEW MARKETS

In addition to grocery stores, Graeter's Ice Cream also turned to shipping to reach markets outside of Ohio and Kentucky.

In the early '90s, the only option for shipping was FedEx because UPS wouldn't accept dry ice, which was necessary to ship ice cream. The problem with FedEx, however, was that its distribution didn't reach everywhere. And the U.S. Postal Service? "They were impossible to work with," Dick said.

In the mid-'90s, everything changed. "Sometime in '94 or '95, [UPS] changed their policy and they started taking dry ice shipments," Dick said. "UPS was the best way to ship to individual homes and things. Distribution was 100 percent of the United States. There were very few places they didn't go."

In 1994, shipping was 0 percent of the family business. Today, it brings in $3 million a year.

TOUGH TRANSITION

The transition of Graeter's Ice Cream from the third generation to the fourth started by accident—literally. In 1989, Jon tumbled down a flight of stairs in a house he was renovating. After a lengthy recovery, he looked at his life, the long hours and hour-long commute from Georgetown every day, and decided it was time to retire. Kathy, who until this point had worked for the company but had not been an owner, bought out his shares.

Jon's accident made the other three siblings, Kathy, Dick and Lou, realize that if they were going to actually transition to the fourth generation any time in the near future, they needed to start working toward that now. That fact was reinforced in 1991 when Wilmer, who had unofficially retired a few years earlier to take care of his ailing wife, died.

But the transition wasn't easy. Dick's son, Richard, came into the business when he was finishing law school at the University of Cincinnati in 1989. He had worked with his uncle Jon at various times, helping with the financials and getting the company's business onto computers. But when Richard originally started in the business after law school, it was an uncomfortable arrangement with his father, Dick. The father-son dynamic seemed to cause rifts within the company.

"When [Jon] left, my son was in law school so he kind of filled in that part of our loss, so to speak," Dick said. "Well, we did get rid of him for a couple of years. We kind of decided he should do something else. We weren't getting along too awful well with everybody." So for a time, Richard went to work with Dinsmore and Shohl, practicing law. (The law firm remains the attorneys for the family business.)

A couple of years later, Dick said, they decided they needed Richard back. "He came back, and he's been with us ever since," Dick said.

Lou's son, Bob, came in about the same time to help organize the plant. "Bob was probably the biggest help to me when he started because there we had to start being more sophisticated in our labeling and all the rules and regulations and purchasing," Dick said.

Kathy worked at getting Chip, Lou's other son, involved in the retail side of the operation, where she had always worked.

BEFORE THEY WERE OWNERS

Richard, Bob and Chip all have memories of working in the Graeter's stores and factories during their youth, though they weren't always sure they would enter the family business as a career choice.

Richard said one of his earliest memories is coming to work with his dad on a Saturday and stamping the ice cream flavors on the lids with a rubber stamp. He also remembers working with his grandpa, Wilmer. "He was very funny. Grandpa

Graeter's Ice Cream at Hyde Park was originally part of Higginson's Tea Room. *Courtesy of Ken Heigel.*

Chip, Bob and Richard Graeter are the fourth generation of Graeters and now run the company. *Courtesy of the Graeter family.*

Ice cream at Graeter's starts with cream, sugar and eggs. *Courtesy of Graeter's Ice Cream.*

Large batches of cream, sugar and eggs are divided into smaller portions to be churned in the French pots, which make just two to three gallons at a time. *Courtesy of Graeter's Ice Cream.*

Melted chocolate is added to the churning ice cream and then scraped into chips in the chocolate chip flavors. *Courtesy of Graeter's Ice Cream.*

Above, clockwise from top left: A sundae at Graeter's includes ice cream, rich bittersweet topping, whipped cream and nuts; The 1870 Tower sundae includes a chocolate bundt cake, ice cream, whipped cream and chopped pecans; A Chip Wheelie sandwich, with ice cream between two chocolate chip cookies. *All images courtesy of Graeter's Ice Cream.*

Opposite, top row, left to right: STRAWBERRY ice cream used to be only seasonal, but it is now offered year-round; PEANUT BUTTER CHIP ice cream is a more recent addition to Graeter's, added to the menu in the 1970s; MOCHA CHIP ice cream is one of Lou Graeter's favorite flavors. *Middle row, left to right*: CHOCOLATE CHIP ice cream is one of the many flavors that include different-size chocolate chunks; When the company first started, CHOCOLATE and vanilla were the only flavors; PEACH ice cream has been part of the Graeter's menu almost from the beginning. *Bottom row, left to right*: DOUBLE CHOCOLATE CHIP combines the luscious chocolate ice cream with rich chunks of chocolate; BLACK CHERRY ice cream is one of the original flavors of Graeter's; BLACK RASPBERRY CHOCOLATE CHIP accounts for 20 percent of all ice cream sales at Graeter's. *All images courtesy of Graeter's Ice Cream.*

This "G" is believed to have come from one of the original stores and is now in the entryway of the Graeter's offices on Reading Road. *Courtesy of Ken Heigel.*

The front of a "tally sheet" from Graeter's, probably from the 1930s. *Courtesy of The History Press.*

Kids of all ages enjoy the ice cream at the Graeter's store on Lane Avenue in Columbus. *Courtesy of Ken Heigel.*

Left: Graeter's ice cream is hand-packed into pints. *Courtesy of Graeter's Ice Cream.*

Below: Pints for sale at the West Chester store sport the new logo. *Courtesy of Ken Heigel.*

always had something going on," Richard said. "At the end of the day you'd be covered with chocolate. But it just seemed normal to me. It's all we ever knew."

For Chip, working in the family business wasn't originally part of his plan, though he had great admiration for his dad, Lou. "He is my true idol," Chip said. "I mean he's amazing."

When he was growing up, he said his father worked long hours but talked very little about the business. Home life, for Chip anyway, was very reminiscent of the '50s television show *Leave It to Beaver*. "My dad worked a lot," he said. "I guess the key was no matter what, I always knew where my bread was buttered so I always had the utmost respect for my dad. I knew he was providing for his family. My mom made that understood to all of us. I had a great childhood."

Still, he wasn't convinced the family business was right for him. He worked as a soda jerk

In the '60s and '70s, and probably before, customers were seated at tables and given menus at Graeter's. *Courtesy of the Cincinnati Historical Museum.*

at different stores during the summer, but it was just that—a summer job. "At that time we waited on tables, so I was the guy who went to your table and brought you a glass of water, a napkin and took your order," he said. "I took it back to the counter. The folks there made it. And I'd deliver it to you and get a fifteen-cent tip, and it was awesome."

But Chip preferred the summers he spent working in maintenance at Graeter's. "It was the best job I ever had at Graeter's. I had a lot of fun," he said. "Every day was something different. I love working with my hands. I love fixing things mechanical. Electrical, plumbing, all kinds of stuff that I've been able to use in my home life."

After he graduated from Wittenberg University in Springfield, Ohio, he was faced with indecision about what he wanted to do next. The university offered him a job in admissions, but on a whim, Chip decided to take a completely different route.

"I was laying out by the pool one day at my mom and dad's condo, talking to this lady. She worked for Delta Airlines in marketing," he said. "She told me I should be a flight attendant." So he filled out an application, got a job interview and three days later left for training in Atlanta. He was a flight attendant for three years. "It was wonderful, wonderful, wonderful," he said.

Richard's sister, Cindy, worked in the family business while in high school and college but became a travel agent after graduation. She now is a stay-at-home mom and a part-time substitute teacher. Lou's remaining child, Mindy, worked at Graeter's for almost two decades after she graduated from college but has since left the family business to become a successful real estate agent.

In 1989, after Jon left the company, Chip's aunt Kathy, with whom he had always been close, came to him and told him if he wanted to get into the business, now was the time. "I always knew someday I'd get back to the business, but I was flying around with young pretty girls all day long. Flying to all these great places and having fun," he said.

Nonetheless, he quit his job as a flight attendant and took over managing the Fourth Street store downtown in the summer of 1989. It wasn't what he expected. "I hated what I was doing. I absolutely hated it," he said, candidly. "Going from carefree, just having fun, having a blast, something different every day to all of a sudden getting there at 6:00 a.m. every day to 5:00 or 6:00 at night, every single day, Monday through Saturday."

But he muddled through one year, married his college sweetheart and began to settle into the family business.

THE FIRST EXPANSION

In 1994, the company decided that it needed to expand the plant facility on Reading Road to accommodate the expanding business into grocery stores.

"I had architects and an engineering firm working on a building in 1990 knowing we needed to expand because we couldn't really handle our business," Dick said. "But Richard didn't feel we were doing well enough to be able to afford to build a building. So we started this addition in '94. Moved here in '95."

The expansion doubled the size of the plant. They added dry storage on the second floor that gave them space to expand the candy room. They doubled the size of the ice cream room and built a freezer five times bigger than the one they had. They added a retail store to the space and expanded the dock area so trucks could actually back in and load up the product directly from the plant.

"We borrowed a lot of money at the time. We went through years and years and didn't borrow any money for equipment or anything. Finally, we did," Dick said. "We borrowed better than

The factory on Reading Road originally did not have a loading dock for trucks such as these. *Courtesy of Ken Heigel.*

An expansion of the factory on Reading Road in 1994 included the addition of a loading dock. *Courtesy of Ken Heigel.*

The expansion of the factory on Reading Road in 1994 included the addition of a store that sells ice cream, baked goods and chocolates. *Courtesy of Ken Heigel.*

a million dollars. At that time for us, that was a lot. [Richard] helped do it. We had to do it. If we were going to be in business, we had to do something. We were busting at the seams." Roughly the same time, Chip's role expanded. He took over the company's number-one grossing store in Kenwood and then worked at bringing in and training good people who could work as district managers, each handling four stores.

"We hired and trained and developed systems and processes. That's kind of where that went for the next couple of years really," he said. "Then in 2001, 2002, we went through that transition."

MAKING THE MOVE

The actual transition of ownership between the generations proved one of the hardest endeavors the family undertook. Part of the problem was figuring out how to equitably sell and gift the ownership of Lou, Dick and Kathy to Richard, Bob and Chip. Richard was Dick's son, Bob and Chip were Lou's sons and Kathy had no children. Plus, Dick and Lou were ready to retire, but Kathy was not.

In an interview with *Business Courier* in 2004, Dick said, "We always felt, starting up in this process, that the only way ultimately it would work was to do it a third, a third, a third. It was very difficult to get my son, who was entitled to half at the time, to agree to that. That was a big problem."

The differences of opinions between one another and the generations on day-to-day operations—what time the stores should open, whether they should buy a new truck, for example—caused conflict, too.

"Transition is always a struggle," Kathy said. "You always have to be thinking ahead to how the future generation is going to fit in." The family began to realize that a successful past didn't guarantee a successful future.

After months of discussing the transition plans with no success, Richard finally offered an ultimatum: get outside help or he would quit the business altogether. And by help, Richard didn't mean more consultants or lawyers. He wanted a family business psychologist.

The Graeters agreed and selected business psychologist Michael Harting at the University of Cincinnati's Goering Center for Family and Private Business to help iron out the plans and work with the feuding personalities. Hartings worked with the family for almost three years, individually and as a group.

The biggest problem, Hartings said in the interview with the *Business Courier*, was that the Graeters lacked a cohesive vision for the future. In addition, they each carried their own issues with the family history.

One thing Hartings emphasized was that the fourth generation had to take a step back from the day-to-day issues and focus on long-term visions for the company. In an interview with *Smart Business*, Richard said the consultants they hired to assist in the transition told them, "If you are out there driving and loading trucks and making ice cream, you can't possibly plan where you want the business to go five or ten years down the road because you're worried about the next five or ten minutes."

The new generation would have to take a broader approach.

At one point, the family divisions looked so cavernous, so impassable, that the family considered splitting the company up, giving Richard the franchises and Bob and Chip the corporation. Ultimately, it wasn't what the family wanted, so they continued to work through their differences. A grave family illness hastened the plan.

Since 2000, Dick had been successfully battling esophageal cancer. But in July 2003, fluid began to build up around his heart. A complication during surgery to drain the fluid caused a serious infection in Dick's lungs. He spent days in intensive care, and for a time, it wasn't clear he would survive. "That made us see how impermanent life is," Richard said.

Upon his recovery, the family was able to put aside its impasses and find suitable solutions to their problems. On December 31, 2003, the transfer of ownership was completed. It would be a new era for Graeter's Ice Cream. When the official legal transition was complete, the third generation had to decide on their new roles. Kathy wasn't ready to retire, so she stayed on to help Chip with the retail business. Lou officially retired but still comes in early every day to help load the trucks with freshly baked goodies to deliver to the stores.

At the beginning, Dick came in every day, too, to offer his opinions and guidance, but it became a source of conflict. "Finally, after two months, I said to him, 'Dad, as long as you are here every day, Chip, Bob and I will never be able to run this place,'" Richard said. "'Yes, we may make mistakes, but we need to make them, learn and move on.'"

Dick agreed and finally fully relinquished his control. Everyone agrees that the process was painful, but the outcome was what they wanted.

"We were smart enough to see we needed outside help," Chip said. "Our fathers worked seventy hours a week in the business, but they didn't set up any kind of transition plan."

Like the third generation before them, the new owners' roles worked out naturally. All three are equal partners: Richard became the CEO, while Chip became the vice-president of retail operations and Bob became the vice-president of production.

Bob and Chip were both happy to relinquish the CEO role to Richard. "Bob and I certainly didn't want it," Chip said of the CEO position. "Rich was an accountant in college, then he got a law degree. He kind of knew what he wanted to do.

Rich's personality is such he's fairly driven in that realm. Rich is much more gregarious and loves that role much more than either of us would."

Chip was happy with his role of heading up the stores.

I always knew I would be in retail. That's where I wanted to be. It had grown on me. I'm very comfortable running our fourteen stores, making sure they're looking good. I'm very focused.

My brother had been in sourcing ingredients and production and a lot of that, taking care of formulations and processes. He is so happy doing what he does. He doesn't want to be out there.

So we all kind of had a niche. It was really a matter of how we would divide the business up.

And all three believe the family is stronger because of the struggles they went through to get to this point. "Today I think we're better than we've ever been. We're together and we're moving forward," Richard said. "Everyone has a piece to contribute. That's really important. We respect each other and trust each other. And like each other. We couldn't say that ten years ago."

Chip agrees. "We traversed through that tumultuous time. But all in all it made us all stronger," he said. "It made us more thankful for each other, eventually. I mean it was terrible at the time. It wasn't really fun. But it was something we had to do."

The benefits now, they all say, are how close the family is and how great it can be to work together. Chip, for example, loves seeing his father and his aunt Kathy every day. Richard said that he and his sister, together with their families, still have Sunday dinner every week with their mom and dad.

NEW LOOK, NEW IDEAS

Once the transition of ownership was complete and the roles were defined, the three new owners had to decide what they wanted to do and where they wanted to take the company. One of the tasks was deciding how Graeter's should appear to the public. "The first thing we did was work on our brand. That was something the three of us all did together," Chip said. "And it was an awesome experience. Something I'd never done before."

While the Graeter's name was well known, the logo itself wasn't necessarily. When the fourth generation took over, the brand logo appeared several different ways in the stores and on products. Over the years, a consistent brand look hadn't been important because the family had been so concerned with the day-to-day operations.

To consolidate the look into one consistent appearance, the company employed Libby Perszyk Kathman Inc., an international brand design agency located in Cincinnati. The company took components from the different logos and created one streamlined version that it incorporated into new packaging. The Graeter's name remained in script typeface, but the pink letters and stripes on a white background were replaced with pale yellows and rich mahoganies, colors that were also used in the development of new stores.

"There is a big difference between [a logo] that has been well thought out and executed and one that has been done on the side, as a secondary product or project over a hundred years. That's what we had. We haven't had a real brand other than the quality of the product," Richard said in an interview with *Smart Business* in 2005.

They also relaunched their website, graeters.com, with the new look and branding—and the ability for customers

The West Chester store, which opened in 2008, shows off the new logo and color scheme. *Courtesy of Ken Heigel.*

from around the country to order ice cream and gift certificates online.

Despite the tough transition between generations, the third generation recognizes the benefits the fourth generation has brought to the company, things they had never done themselves. "I think they're doing a lot better job in marketing and advertising," Lou said.

Dick agrees. "We just didn't do that. I think our generation was pretty old-fashioned," he said. "We did a little advertising but we always felt the product sold itself. Any new stores now have a lot of the same features as the other stores, where for years we just put a store up. We just made it fit the community or whatever. There was no continuity of branding or whatever. Now they really have stepped that up."

Part of the changes and expansions have been necessary to keep the family business in the family. "We sold enough to make a good living for our family. Then of course we got more family. And we had to do more," Dick said.

Part of doing more means deciding what products to keep, including different ice cream flavors, based on sales. "There were flavors that came and went. If it did well, we kept it," Dick said. "This group does everything by the numbers. If it sells 1 percent, they drop it."

His son, Richard, doesn't disagree. "We don't keep as many unpopular flavors anymore." Richard and Dick didn't always agree on what flavors to bring to market, either. When Ben & Jerry's introduced cookie dough ice cream in the '80s, it became so popular with consumers that other ice cream makers started imitating it within months. But Dick wasn't interested in making a Graeter's version of cookie dough or cookies and cream, another popular flavor of the time, because they were what he called "popular" flavors. Richard saw an advantage in making Graeter's versions of these flavors, and he saw them through to market.

"Cookie dough ice cream made *our* way with *our* chocolate chips. And our cookies and cream made our way, which is buying whole Oreos instead of itty-bitty broken pieces," Richard said. "They're some of our bestsellers still."

Richard also points out that while Dick has strong opinions about Graeter's Ice Cream flavors, he isn't the company's ideal customer. The majority of Graeter's customers are kids and moms.

In addition to a new physical look, the three new owners took a long-term look at the company and their goals. Richard, Chip and Bob hired consultants Robin Guiler and Paul Porcino, who had decades of business experience at Procter & Gamble and Lens Crafters, respectively. Guiler and Porcino facilitated a series of retreats in 2007 that helped Richard, Chip and Bob come up with a mission, core values and strategic direction, something that most companies start with when they're formed but that the Graeters had never set down.

The mission is simple: "To make the best ice cream you have ever tasted." It is, Richard says, more than a phrase that hangs in a frame on the wall. It's what the Graeters go back to over and over every time they want to make a company decision.

With the mission in place, they came up with core values: 1) their heritage, 2) their products, 3) their customers, 4) their employees and 5) their community.

For strategic directions, the trio agreed on: 1) to create and maintain a professionally run company with sustainable profitability, 2) to develop and sustain a highly qualified, performing employee base, 3) to improve the Graeter's experience through people and facilities, 4) to optimize the Cincinnati operating company and 5) to exploit the growth potential of the brand in new geographic markets.

With all of these foundations in place, it was easy to see on what areas the company needed to focus its attention.

One of the first was with employees. First, Richard, Bob and Chip brought Guiler and Porcino on as full-time consultants in crucial roles in the company. In an article in *Smart Business*, Richard said, "In the past, you had the employee members and you had Graeters, and that was that. There was no in between."

Guiler and Porcino fill a gap, bringing talents to the company that Richard, Bob and Chip don't have. Under Guiler's and Porcino's guidance, the company embarked on training programs that gave employees, from managers to part-time store workers, the skills they needed to succeed. When employees completed training, they were eligible for raises and promotions. In addition, all workers are offered paid days off and health insurance.

"We have employees that have stayed with us for their lifetime," Richard said. The fourth generation wanted to keep that momentum while also giving the employees a chance to succeed and grow.

Another area that required attention was production efficiency. To improve it, Graeter's started running three shifts of ice cream making instead of two. They worked out a schedule of workers so they never had to shut down during a shift. They dedicated certain crew members to clean up and tear down. They became diligent about maintenance, to keep the machines operating at top form all the time. The improvements were dramatic.

"The year I started in the business we were making 100,000 gallons," Richard said. "In 2004, we were making 200,000."

In 2007, Richard also expanded relationships with his dairy suppliers, Trauth Dairy of Newport, Kentucky, and Smith Dairy of Orville, Ohio, turning them into distributors of Graeter's Ice Cream. Now, along with other brands, the dairies, as well as UDF, include Graeter's Ice Cream in their trucks delivering ice cream to various locations.

"Distribution was a competency we did not have. You have to know what you're doing," Richard said. "When you're only a niche product, it is almost impossible to develop the necessary distribution system. At one time, my bakery drivers would drop off product at the country club while delivering."

Now, the dairies, along with UDF trucks, distribute Graeter's to grocery stores.

All the changes and transitions set the family on the path for a brighter future.

LOOKING TO THE FUTURE

Today, Cincinnati houses a population of more than 300,000 and more than 2 million people if surrounding areas are included. It is the third largest city in Ohio, behind Cleveland and Columbus. It is home to numerous businesses, including Procter & Gamble, Kroger, Federated Department Stores (owner of Macy's and Bloomingdale's) and Chiquita Brands International.

Over the years, the city has been the birthplace of many famous—and some infamous—people, including abolitionist Harriet Beecher Stowe, entertainer Doris Day, film director Steven Spielberg, crooner Rosemary Clooney, pop singer Nick Lachey, talk-show host Jerry Springer, disgraced Cincinnati Reds player and coach Pete Rose and mass murderer Charles Manson.

Cincinnati was the home of one of the worst rock concert tragedies in U.S. history, when eleven fans were killed and dozens injured in a rush for seating at a sold-out concert by The Who at Riverfront Coliseum in 1979.

The city again drew national attention when the Robert Mapplethorpe photo exhibit opened at the Contemporary Arts Center in 1990 and its director, Dennis Barrie, was indicted on obscenity charges because of the graphic sexual nature of the photographs. Barrie was acquitted of the charges later that year, though the trial brought the question of what constitutes art to the national forefront.

Race relations remained an ongoing challenge for the city. Riots broke out in 2001 after an unarmed black man was shot, and the police department was accused of racial profiling. Many people feel these riots cost the city its bid to host the 2012 Summer Olympics.

At the same time, however, the National Underground Railroad Freedom Museum honoring the city's important work on the Underground Railroad was being planned. It opened in 2004, and to date, it has brought in almost one million visitors from across the country and around the globe.

Cincinnati Reds owner Marge Schott, who died in 2004, caused her own race relation debacles over and over in the '90s with her racist comments and professed admiration of Adolf Hitler. These views led to her one-year suspension by Major League Baseball and overshadowed her acts of kindness and generosity.

Beloved Riverfront Stadium was demolished in 2002 to make way for a new ballpark. The Great American Ball Park, where the Reds play, opened a year later, built next to the site where Riverfront had stood. It is smaller than Riverfront, seating just over forty-two thousand, but is praised for its breathtaking views and innovative features, including Italian marble mosaics and a riverboat deck, as well as its tribute to Reds' history.

The Cincinnati Bengals, who had shared Riverfront with the Reds, got their own new football stadium down the street: Paul Brown Stadium, named for the team's original owner.

Paul Brown holds sixty-five thousand people. The Astroturf of Riverfront has been replaced with FieldTurf, an artificial surface that more closely mimics natural grass. The Bengals, who went to the Super Bowl twice in the '80s, have yet to win the World Championship.

Through the decades, Cincinnati has also developed its own food culture, including Skyline Chili, which started in 1949 and serves its thin chili (with more aromatic spices than fiery heat) over spaghetti or on hot dogs topped with a cyclone of thinly shredded cheddar cheese. La Rosa's Pizza, with its sweet tomato sauce and crispy crust, started in 1954 and has become an institution, as has Montgomery Inn, known for its fall-from-the-bone, sweet-smoky barbecued ribs. The restaurant started in Montgomery north of Cincinnati in 1951 and now has a location on the Ohio River downtown, as well as one in nearby Fort Mitchell, Kentucky, and Dublin, a suburb of Columbus. (By the way, Montgomery Inn serves Graeter's Ice Cream for dessert.)

Through it all, the Queen City has remained home to Graeter's Ice Cream, one of the oldest family-owned ice cream businesses in the country.

The company still offers eight "original flavors," including black cherry, coffee, strawberry and butter pecan, and a handful of sorbet flavors, such as strawberry. In addition, Graeter's makes ten of its ever-popular chocolate chip flavors, including Buckeye Blitz, toffee chocolate chip and, of course, the customer favorite, black raspberry chocolate chip. Seasonal flavors such as pumpkin, cinnamon, peach and tangerine rotate in and out during certain months.

The retail stores continue to offer many of the same sodas, milkshakes and sundaes they've made for nearly one hundred years. Now there's also a signature sundae commemorating the company's history: the 1870 Tower. It features a chocolate bundt cake filled with hot fudge and a scoop of

The oldest Graeter's store in Cincinnati sits on Hyde Park Square. *Courtesy of Ken Heigel.*

The West Chester store combines the new look and feel with the same old-fashioned charm. *Courtesy of Ken Heigel.*

black raspberry chocolate chip ice cream, drizzled with more hot fudge and then topped off with whipped cream, chopped pecans and a cherry.

In the Cincinnati area, Graeter's Ice Cream has fourteen retail stores. In Kentucky there are fourteen stores plus two in Indiana, owned by two franchises. The Columbus area has eleven stores, plus another four that the same franchise opened in Dayton. One Columbus store and two Dayton locations are housed in the same building as another Ohio favorite: City Barbecue.

In all, there are a total of forty-five retail operations, plus its ever-expanding online business. In recent years, Graeter's Ice Cream has also started dabbling in social media, including Twitter and Facebook, which has a fan page with more than fifty-five thousand fans and encourages customers to post photos of the biggest chocolate chips they've found in the ice cream.

Going forward, Graeter's Ice Cream, like any small family business, will be beset with challenges. One of them, however, is not the recession that hit the country hard in 2008. "I think it's been so dramatic," said Richard Graeter, fourth generation and current CEO of the company, "but it has not affected us dramatically."

Louisville franchisee Jim Tedesko agrees. "The recession in a sense helped our business. In 2009, we had our best year ever," he said. Tedesko suspects it was because consumers were willing to spend a little extra money on good ice cream that had the added bonus of being locally produced.

Richard points out that being somewhat recession-proof has been something of a hallmark of Graeter's. Even during the Great Depression, Graeter's endured and even expanded. "You'll pinch pennies, maybe not go out for dinner. But ice cream is happy. You can take the family out for ice cream and for a dollar or two more have the best of the best."

STIFF COMPETITION

The ice cream market is more competitive than ever. While sales of ice cream in the United States are expected to grow from $24.6 billion to $26.5 billion by 2014, overall the market is considered fairly saturated. The per capita rate of consumption of ice cream has gone down from 22 quarts in 2001 to 20.1 quarts in 2009.

Few truly new innovations have come to market, with the exception of Dippin' Dots, small beads of ice cream flash-frozen in liquid nitrogen. They were introduced in 1991 and have become popular at malls and sports venues but remain a relatively small part of the market. Mix-in stores, such as Cold Stone Creamery and Marble Slab, are another niche market in the ice cream business.

Frozen yogurt is starting to make a strong return with the introduction of new soft serve frozen yogurt shops such as Pinkberry and Red Mango. Sales growth of ice cream didn't quite reach 3 percent from 2005 to 2009, but frozen yogurt sales grew almost 9 percent during the same period. But in the frozen dessert market, ice cream remains king. The ice cream market can still be divided into four categories: economy (low milk fat, high overrun), regular (higher quality but still bargain-priced), premium (higher milk fat and lower overrun; includes branded and private labels) and super-premium (with high milk fat and very low overrun). In addition, a new category, known as artisan, now exists. Many cities have local ice cream makers turning out fine products, such as Madisono's Gelato in Cincinnati and Jeni's Splendid Ice Cream in Columbus.

Richard says that artisan products, however, are a different niche in the ice cream market than Graeter's. In fact, he thinks Graeter's doesn't truly fit into any of the categories. "Graeter's is a niche in and of itself," he said.

The company is still family owned, the ice cream is made the old-fashioned way and, unlike Jeni's with its exotic flavors such as Cherry Lambic and Salty Caramel, Graeter's flavors are "good, old American flavors." The most exotic flavor at Graeter's, Richard says, is the black raspberry chocolate chip, which also happens to be the company's number-one seller.

Manufacturers of all kinds of ice cream compete fiercely for space in the grocery store freezer. The two biggest super-premium brands remain Häagen Dazs (owned by Nestle) and Ben & Jerry's (owned by Unilever). Together, Nestle and Uniliver own roughly 44 percent of the entire U.S. ice cream market. National brands have deep marketing pockets and snazzier packaging to achieve name recognition with consumers. These companies can also attach to trends quickly, as in the reduced-fat ice cream market.

A health and wellness revolution has caused ice cream producers to add ingredients with perceived health benefits, such as probiotics and omega-3 oils, to their ice cream so they can tout the "healthfulness" of their ice cream. Another trend continues to be the removal of "bad" ingredients such as fat and sugar. National brands, as well as other Ohio ice cream producers such as Pierre's in Cleveland and Velvet Ice Cream in Utica near Columbus, have capitalized on the low-fat segment by adding more flavors of their "slow-churned," low-fat varieties. A half-cup serving of Edy's Slow-Churned ice cream (Edy's is owned by Nestle and sold in western states as Dreyer's) contains a little more than a third of the calories and a quarter of the fat of a half-cup serving of Graeter's.

Most commercial ice creams already use industrial ingredients that mimic the luxurious mouthfeel from butterfat and eggs, which are too costly and too perishable to add on a large scale. Some of the ingredients are natural, like carrageenan, which is extracted from algae. Others, including mono- and di-glycerides, are synthetic.

Some of these ice creams, such as Edy's, use so much of these stabilizing ingredients that it actually prohibits them from melting, as ice cream should. In an article in *Cook's Illustrated* magazine comparing supermarket vanilla ice creams, Edy's Grand Vanilla was not recommended because of its "fluffy, marshmallow-y texture." The editors also noticed that when left sitting at room temperature for twenty minutes, it didn't melt. (Graeter's was not included in this comparison because, while it is sold at supermarkets, it is not a national brand.)

When it comes to low-fat ice cream, the newest ingredient is a manufactured version of a protein found in fish, along with a low-temperature extrusion process that increases the creaminess of low-fat ice creams. But these ingredients are not ones Graeter's will even consider. The ingredients in Graeter's Ice Cream remain just cream, sugar, eggs and flavorings. The low-fat segment remains one in which Graeter's refuses to compete. "No. Emphatically, no," said Richard about adding a low-fat line to the mix. "That's just not ice cream. Dessert is an indulgence. Have a reasonable portion for dessert and take a walk."

Richard believes in "real" food, the kind preached by well-known author and food philosopher Michael Pollan, who has written books such as *The Omnivore's Dilemma*, *In Defense of Food* and *Food Rules*. Graeter's does not, Richard says, give the "slow-churned" varieties a second thought. "They're using technology and stabilizers and ingredients to try to give the mouthfeel of a full fat product without being one. I would rather just have cream, sugar and eggs."

Graeter's has always, however, offered no-fat fruit sorbets that are truly just remnants of the very first ices before cream was introduced. For a short time in the '90s, the company also had a line of low-glycemic ice creams at the retail stores, but they were not aimed at cashing in on diet fads. "We did experiment with low-glycemic, not for diet reasons, but for diabetics," Richard said. "It was pretty good. Diabetics loved it."

Unfortunately, the supply of the sweetener that they used in place of sugar because it did not cause sugar levels in the blood to spike was not reliably available. "We decided it was not our niche," Richard said, though he noted that he wouldn't mind having a low-glycemic offering if they could find the right ingredients to make it.

Nonetheless, locally, Graeter's has done very well in Kroger stores in the Cincinnati area. Krogers sells more Graeter's Ice Cream than Häagen-Dazs and Ben & Jerry's—and at some stores more than both of them combined. Cincinnati is the only place in the country, possibly in the world, where those two internationally known super-premium ice creams are not number one and two in sales at grocery stores.

Unlike other companies, Graeter's holds back on promoting one of the biggest strengths of its product: that it's all-natural. It's obvious in the ingredient list, but it's stamped in only small letters on the lids of the pints. "We've been careful to make a quality, all-natural product without trying to hype it," Richard said.

Häagen-Dazs, on the other hand, released a new line of ice creams called Häagen-Dazs Five, emphasizing that each one contained only five ingredients. The catch? The majority of its ice creams, aside from those with candy or cookie pieces, had always had just five ingredients. The "new" line of ice cream was little more than a marketing ploy.

A PLAN AND A PLANT

To compete with all of the different ice creams currently on the market, Graeter's has decided to take its ice cream into new markets outside of Ohio and Kentucky. But instead of opening more retail stores, they'll be selling pints at more grocery stores. To cover the product needed to move Graeter's into more markets from Denver to Houston to Atlanta, in 2009 the company announced plans to build a new plant. The twenty-eight-thousand-square-foot facility located in the Bond Hill area of Cincinnati is scheduled for completion in mid-2010.

The plant is necessary, the third generation says. "They're marketing faster than they've got room to support it—ice cream wise, I mean," Dick said.

When plans for the new plant were announced, in the midst of the recession, the city of Cincinnati was especially pleased.

"Graeter's is a Cincinnati institution," said Mayor Mark Mallory. "It is exciting to see one of our hometown, family companies grow and succeed."

The city has also put its money behind the expansion, offering Graeter's a 4.5-acre parcel on which to build the plant as well as a low-interest loan to fund the construction. When the expansion is complete, the company will go from having fourteen ice cream machines that can make 300,000 gallons of ice cream a year when the plant is at full production to double that with an additional ten machines plus room to expand capacity to up to 1.5 million gallons a year.

Another big change is the new plant's shrink-wrap facility for packaging—something that used to be done by United Dairy Farmers—and a large freezer to store ice cream after it's made. This means the ice cream can get to the far-away stores in a matter of days. Unlike mass-produced ice cream, which may be as much as a year old by the time it hits the supermarket freezer shelves, Graeter's is just weeks, maybe even days, old.

"It's an exciting time," said Chip. "It's either the smartest thing we ever did or our kids may hate us forever, if we laden them with this huge factory. It's a great product. And I think people will want us in other places, too. That's what we're betting on."

But some things in the new plant won't change at all. The new machines will run virtually the same way as the old ones, churning out just two to three gallons at a time. And the raw ingredients won't change at all. The dairy products for the ice cream will still come from Trauth Dairy in Newport, Kentucky, and from Smith Dairy in Orville. Vanilla beans will be ground with sugar before being mixed in for the vanilla flavor. Strawberries and peaches will be added at the beginning of the freezing process so that they will be broken down into smaller pieces for those two popular seasonal flavors. And the black raspberries for the company's number one flavor will be pureed, the seeds removed and then cooked down and sweetened to intensify its flavor and color. None of that will change.

Richard said when he started with the company in 1989 it was a $5 million company, freezing 100,000 gallons of ice cream a year. When he and his cousins took over in 2004, they froze 200,000 gallons. In 2010, it will be a $35 million company when all the franchises are included, producing 300,000 gallons of ice cream each year, fifteen times the production of twenty years ago. "We have seen steady growth for the last one hundred years. We're probably on the cusp of an atypical growth," Richard said.

Nonetheless, by national standards Graeter's is still small. Pierre's, another family-owned one-hundred-year-old Ohio ice cream company was worth $37 million in 2007. At its peak in 1982, Häagen-Dazs sold sixty-five million pints a year and was worth $115 million before it was sold to the Pillsbury Corporation in 1983. Ben & Jerry's, before it was taken over by Unilever in 1998, was worth $237 million.

Richard also points out that, like Ben & Jerry's, Graeter's has always been a good corporate citizen; it just doesn't trumpet its social mission. "Every good decent ethical company should behave in a decent way. You pay a fair wage, good benefits, use the best ingredients," Richard said. "We're involved in charities, public radio. We've done it for one hundred years. We just don't turn it into a marketing gimmick."

Despite the excitement of the new plant and anticipated growth, both the third and fourth generations enter into the new decade with guarded concern. "I'm excited about it but there's still quite a bit of trepidation. I'm still very nervous," Chip said. "We're still a very small business really. Ben & Jerry's and Häagen-Dazs could crush us easily. Our product is still so handmade and hand crafted. Can it handle going beyond our little border? Our little area? I think so."

Kathy believes it can, too, as long as the company maintains the ice cream as it is. "We have to be very careful about it and make sure the product maintains its integrity," she said. "I'm confident we can do that. I think this is a good direction to be going. The markets we're going in have had some exposure to the product, and so far it's been accepted."

Franchisee Jim Tedesko feels more ambivalent about the expansion. "I think it's good. It will bring brand awareness on a national level," he said. "But on the other hand, it's kind of nice that we're local and unique."

Tedesko says many people in Louisville bring out-of-town guests to the Graeter's Ice Cream shops for something locally produced. "If everyone can get it, it's not as special of a treat."

A SPECIAL CONTRIBUTION

Graeter's Ice Cream has undertaken a fair amount of charity work, including the development of a new flavor for a special little girl.

In 2006, the Desserich family of Cincinnati received devastating news: Their five-year-old daughter, Elena, was diagnosed with brainstem glioma, a deadly form of pediatric brain cancer. She died a few months later.

The Desseriches were determined not to let their daughter's death be in vain, so they set up a foundation, The Cure Starts Now, to educate, aid and fund the research for a cure for pediatric brain cancer. As part of their first gala fundraiser, they approached the Graeters for a contribution.

Richard said the Graeter family was touched by the story and offered to sell the opportunity for one person to create a new ice cream flavor in Elena's name. The ice cream would then be sold at the retail outlets for one month, and a percentage of the profits would go to The Cure Starts Now.

The flavor, Elena's Blueberry Pie Ice Cream, went on sale in July 2008. It sold out in two weeks. "We had to scramble to make more," Richard said.

The Graeters decided to make Elena's Blueberry Pie Ice Cream a permanent flavor, available by the scoop and by the pint at retail stores, select grocery stores and at their website, with a portion of the proceeds continuing to go to the fund. In 2009, Graeter's donated $15,000 to The Cure Starts Now. In addition to helping to raise more funds, they sell the Desseriches' book, *Notes Left Behind*, which is filled with the drawings and notes Elena left for her family in the months before she died, tucked into books on the bookshelf, between the dishes in the china cabinet and in briefcases and backpacks.

BAKED GOODS AND CHOCOLATE

Despite the bright future for the ice cream, the future of the candy and bakery business remains in limbo.

"The candy business and bakery business have remained flat. We're really just trying to make it reasonably profitable in those areas," Dick said. "We lost so much money that the ice cream business has carried the bakery business."

The family is divided on what to do with the bakery and chocolate business, which is only available in the retail stores in Cincinnati owned by the family. Richard would like to see it go away, but Kathy wants it to remain. While Dick recognizes the bottom line, he also feels the bakery adds something to the Graeter's stores that customers can't find elsewhere.

"It lends a lot of mystique to our retail stores that you don't have at other stores," Dick said. "Our stores are pretty neat

Glass cases at Graeter's in West Chester are filled with chocolate confections and fresh-baked cakes and pastries. *Courtesy of Ken Heigel.*

stores. They're confectionary stores. You can find these three really really good products that you can't find somewhere else. We don't necessarily convince all the people of that all the time, but it is true."

Richard takes a more logical approach. "I think we have a really great bakery," he said. "The problem with the bakery line isn't the product. The problem is people have changed their shopping patterns. They don't go to stores anymore to get bakery products. They can get it at grocery stores. They can get it at the gas station. Either get people to your store or you need to take your products to them."

Richard hopes to develop a line of Graeter's bakery products that could be sold in the freezer section of grocery stores, something customers could warm or bake at home that would be different, and perhaps even better, than what they can even get at Graeter's stores now.

The candy business, which has been a part of Graeter's since its inception, presents similar challenges. Kathy loves the chocolates, so much so that she'll only allow herself to eat the filled Easter eggs after the holiday for fear that she would eat too many of them every day if she had that unlimited supply.

But Graeter's hardly has an exclusive edge on the candy market. "Wholesale candy is a very competitive business," Richard said. "There are a lot of big candy companies: Ester Price, Russell Stover." Richard feels he can't compete with them, even though he knows his chocolate is better than both.

The new plant, he says, will focus strictly on ice cream, and, for now, candy and bakery items will still be produced at the Reading Road facility.

GENERATIONAL CONTRIBUTIONS

In looking toward the future, the fourth generation also is mindful of what previous generations brought to the business. "Each generation has its contribution," Richard said.

The first generation created and then expanded the ice cream business. The second generation expanded to the bakery business. The third generation reinvested in the current business, closing stores that weren't profitable, expanding into franchising and getting into supermarkets.

"My dad, my two uncles and Kathy ran the business twenty or thirty years," Chip said. "They made sure they didn't take a lot out of the business, and neither do we. We're making sure we can pass it on to the next generation."

Richard agrees. "We inherited a business, or purchased a business, I should say, that was significantly better off than the one they inherited," Richard said of his father, aunt and uncles.

"Our contribution is what's happening now, the next plant," Richard said. "We're working with Kroger to sell Graeter's in other cities. Shipper business, getting ice cream over the Internet came up. Some things you keep the same, like the ice cream. Some things you change, like your store locations."

"I don't see shrinking our retail footprint, but I don't see building fifty more stores," Richard said.

Right now, 60 percent of the business is retail, 20 percent shipping and 20 percent grocery. With the projected expansion into new markets, Richard said in ten years he sees grocery sales being 50 percent of the family business. But he'll keep some products exclusive to the retail stores, partly to keep customers coming back but, again, as a matter of practicality.

"We do what we call bonus flavors, flavors just in our stores, something special that you have to come to Graeter's to get versus something you can get at Kroger," Richard said. "A flavor has got to really hit it big to make it to Kroger now. Because we have to invest a lot. The development of the flavor is the easy part. The art, the packaging, all of that? That costs thousands of dollars, and it can take a year."

The family says there are no more plans for additional franchises, either. "They have been successful, but at the same time you have a lot less control of the product," Kathy said.

In fact, in June 2010, Graeter's Ice Cream bought back the Columbus and Dayton franchises owned by Maury Levine and Clay Cookery. The office in Cincinnati now operates all of the Ohio stores. While the Graeters were happy with the franchises, they saw the purchase as an opportunity to build the relationships with Columbus and Dayton customers. Richard also says buying back the franchise helped the family maintain control of the product and the brand.

We don't want other people making our ice cream. Franchises really at the end of the day are all about franchising. I mean, whether it's ice cream or pizza or tacos. When you make franchises it's about growth, growth, growth. You lose control of it. Usually, the brand gets destroyed in the process.

We were at a point a couple of years ago where we asked, do we sell twenty new franchisees and teach them how to make ice cream and send them out into the world? Or do we take the risk and invest the money in ourselves in making a new ice cream plant to make more ice cream to supply Kroger? And that's what we decided to do.

When moving into ownership of the company, Richard knew it couldn't stay exactly the same and survive. "Growth can be your enemy. People say you have to grow or die. That's not entirely true to me," Richard said. "We could have stayed as is for a while. But you can only do that if you keep the group small. Our challenge is to grow at a pace where we don't lose what's most important, which is the quality of the product."

And like the generations before them, this generation is doing more than making a living for themselves. "We're custodians for our turn. It's our job to make it better, to keep it in the family," Richard said. "Part of what I think is if you set up your kids with a big pot of money in a trust fund somewhere, what kind of life is that? But if you leave them a business that requires effort to keep going, you get a better person out of that. I think we all share the same sentiment."

Chip echoes that idea: "We'd still like to keep it a family business. I want my kids to do whatever they want to, of course, but that opportunity will be there for them, that's the idea."

Richard said he's received many offers from people wanting to buy the company. But unlike other small ice cream manufacturers that eventually sold to large corporations, the

The fifth generation of Graeters enjoys the fruits of the family business.
Courtesy of Graeter's Ice Cream.

Graeters want to keep the company in the family. "If I had a nickel for every offer, I'd be rich," he said. "We have never seriously considered an offer."

Kathy is proud of where the business has been and where it's going. "I think it's great heritage to have something that's been in your family for 140 years this year," she said. "A pretty amazing event actually."

ACCOLADES

Even without the expansion efforts, Graeter's Ice Cream is reaching a wider market than ever, to a great degree on the wings of all the positive press.

Talk show and magazine mogul Oprah Winfrey was brief but complimentary in the recommendation of Graeter's from her magazine in 2002: "You haven't tried ice cream till you've had Graeter's. The butter pecan is Stedman's favorite, and mine, too." Winfrey also talked about Graeter's on her television show the same year. The day after she mentioned Graeter's, the company shipped four hundred boxes of ice cream to people all over the country—up substantially from the forty they usually ship.

In June 2004, *Cincinnati* magazine declared Graeter's black raspberry chocolate chip ice cream one of the foods that "define" the city, along with Virginia Bakery Schnecken, Trauth Dairy's Sour Cream and Kroeger & Sons Sausages. Here's what the magazine wrote about Graeter's:

How do you make great ice cream? Ask any member of the Graeter's family, and they'll tell you the same way they've been making it since 1870—in small batches, in a "French pot" freezer, with the best ingredients available... The careful tending produces a particularly dense product, perhaps the reason why a pint of Graeter's will serve four handily.

For the crème de la crème, I nominate the black raspberry chip, the closest thing to a transcendent experience ice cream can provide. What makes it so good? It could be the sensation of the rich, frozen cream giving way to the warmth of chocolate melting on your tongue. Or perhaps the dark chocolate chips, hidden like little icebergs in the magenta-colored ice cream. Then there's the intense flavor of black raspberries, tasting like they were distilled from their natural state to something better. But I'm betting that it's not any one thing, but a delicate balance: the slight bitterness of the chocolate complementing the fresh sweetness of the berry, which has just enough tartness to keep things interesting.

David Rosengarten, award-winning food writer and former restaurant critic for *Gourmet* magazine, declared Graeter's the best ice cream in his wildly popular newsletter. He originally had given the honor to a small restaurant in New York in 2002, leaving Graeter's out. He was overwhelmed with letters asking how he could not pick Graeter's. Here's what he wrote in a follow-up piece in 2005:

Simple: I'd never tasted it, even though it was founded in 1870. But I'm sure glad those folks wrote to me, because now I've tasted it—and I'll never leave it out again! This is heartland ice cream at its best, enriched with eggs—absolutely winning waves of dairy, which is the best feature of Graeter's Ice Cream.

Take the vanilla. Forget the Tahitian stuff; this ice cream tastes like the best vanilla milk shake you ever had at the soda shoppe, or like the last licks of concentrated milk in the bottom of a particularly great bowl of cereal. The lightish-beige chocolate, which is not chocolate freaks' chocolate, but a killer blend of fudgescicle taste and big ice cream impact, is superb. There's a little candy bar and Dixie cup chocolate in there as well.

The reddish-pink strawberry, with its little flecks of seeds and fruit, is a platonic blend of huge cream and good fruit, which trickles down your throat like nostalgia.

But the two best ice creams I tasted from Graeter's were the other flavors they sent. Is this the best black cherry ice cream ever? I think so—with the almost winy, alcoholic richness of the enormous cherry chunks meeting the usual creamy orgasm. Lots of people put "stuff" in ice cream, but I could see immediately that Graeter's basic formula makes it ideal for mixing with "stuff." That was sure the case in the knock-out toffee chip, which bombards you with creamy, buttery, nutty, caramelly chocolate sensations, wrapped of course, in that Ohio cream thing.

In June 2006, Christopher Buckley of forbes.com, a self-declared ice cream snob, wrote about growing up on Good Humor and Carvel soft serve and how, in adulthood, he branched out to find the best of the sweet treat he could. He thought he had discovered the pinnacle at the University Pastry Shop in the Cleveland Park neighborhood of Washington,

D.C., where he lived (he was also a fan of the much ballyhooed Berthillon and Dallyou in Paris). After tasting Graeter's Ice Cream, however, he realized that the best ice cream was in an unlikely location.

A few years ago, a dear friend from Ohio confided— rather insisted—that the best ice cream in the world is made in Cincinnati, by a firm called Graeter's. Ice cream snob that I am, I treated this revelation with skepticism and hauteur. Cincinnati? Well, all right, if you say so…

She turned out to be right. Never have I more gladly eaten my words than when I fell—free-falling—into that first pint of Graeter's black raspberry chip. Why, I demanded, had no one told me of this before? To have wasted a half-century! I dug deeper, into their peach, strawberry, coffee, caramel, double chocolate chip, mint chocolate chip, eggnog. How ironic, how delicious, how patriotic, to have traveled the world in search of happiness only to find it—in Cincinnati.

Money magazine did a fun piece in 2006 where it had four pregnant women taste five ice creams that could be mail-ordered from anywhere in the country. Graeter's black raspberry chocolate chip came in second only to Il Aboratorio Del Gelato from New York and beat Columbus's Jeni's Splendid Ice Creams salty caramel flavor. The tasters said it was sweet and complex, nice and smooth, "the way ice cream from childhood tasted."

In December 2005, *Vanity Fair* magazine recommended Graeter's as one of its "hot gifts," saying that Graeter's was "one of the best homemade-ice-cream companies in the country."

The company was written about not once but twice by *Saveur* magazine, first when the magazine wrote:

> *Ice cream artisans have a long history in this country (New York shopkeeper Philip Lindsay first marketed his flavors in 1777), and today, great ice cream is easy to find—locally…Graeter's quest for good fruit symbolizes* [Dick Graeter's] *dedication: His fussy search for prime peaches starts in the Carolinas in midsummer and moves north with the season, paying off with fresh peach ice cream. Earlier in the summer, he scours Oregon and Washington for black raspberries to go in his best selling flavor, black raspberry chip. But his biggest triumph is the chocolate chips.*

The magazine again wrote about it in a roundup of ice cream parlors across the country. Graeter's was named along with Amy's Ice Creams in Austin, Texas, Dr. Bob's Handcrafted Ice Creams in Upland, California, and Ted Drewes Frozen Custard in St. Louis.

When Ben Cohen, co-founder of Ben & Jerry's Ice Cream, was asked by *USA Today* for his favorite ice cream parlors in July 2002, he listed Graeter's as one of the best.

Gourmet magazine was also a fan of Graeter's, describing it as "the perfect pint."

And finally, *Chicago* magazine said Graeter's was a must for those taking a road trip to the Queen City:

> *From an endless array of choices, we picked a bowl of mocha chocolate chip with marshmallows and hot chocolate sauce, that was smooth, rich, and insanely creamy. It was about here that my wife, a lifelong Chicagoan asked how much I thought a house in Cincinnati cost.*

The Graeter family also says it has received orders from a number of celebrities, including Sarah Jessica Parker, George Clooney (his aunt, Rosemary Clooney, was a long-standing family friend of the Graeters; she also became the celebrity spokesperson for Graeter's when the Aronoff Center store opened downtown in 1996), Nick Lachey, Kevin Costner, Ashley Judd and Justin Timberlake.

In addition, Graeter's is the official ice cream of the Cincinnati Bengals.

TIMELINE

1868–1872
Louis Charles Graeter leaves home in Indiana for the big city and begins selling ice cream at a street market, eventually establishing a storefront on Sycamore Street.

1873–1883
Louis and his brother Fred move to various storefronts, adding candy to the business and eventually following the incline up to Walnut Hills. In August 1883, Louis leaves to open an ice cream company in California.

1900–1918
Louis returns to Cincinnati, marries Regina Berger and resumes operating Graeter's Ice Cream in Walnut Hills (which his brother continued during his absence). The couple settles at 967 East McMillan Street.

1919

Louis dies in a tragic accident. Regina continues the business with her two young sons.

The Roaring Twenties

Regina begins opening satellite stores, beginning with Walnut Street downtown and the Higginson's Tea Room in Hyde Park. Six new stores are opened by 1929.

World War II

Underperforming stores are closed or relocated, and Graeter's enjoys a period of high profitability as war-weary customers enjoy sweet treats at Graeter's during a time of rationing.

Postwar Years

Ice cream industry begins to change with the introduction of soft serve and home freezers that make packaged ice cream feasible at home all year round.

1955

Regina Graeter, "the Boss," dies; business is carried on by her sons, Wilmer and Paul. The industry changes from mom and pop shops to an era of big commercial dairies and mass production.

1957

Bakery product line is introduced in response to competitive challenges of new soft serve and the trend to eat ice cream at home.

1958–1980s

Wilmer, with sons Louis, Dick and Jon, buys out Uncle Paul and rebuilds a business that had deteriorated due to lack of investment over the previous decade.

1981
Graeter's opens prototype single-store ice cream factory on Colerain Avenue based on new Carpigiani batch freezer.

1984
Graeter's first franchise operation opens in northern Kentucky. Single-store factory concept is abandoned, but the Carpigiani machines prove successful.

1987
Graeter's begins selling ice cream through Kroger.

1989
Fourth-generation Chip, Bob and Richard join the business.

1995
Plant expansion is completed, nearly doubling the space to twenty-five thousand square feet at a cost of almost $2 million.

2004
Transition of ownership to the fourth generation is completed. Major brand projects completed, resulting in a professional brand mark, packaging and environmental designs.

2005–2007
Work begins to add three new retail stores, taking Graeter's outside Hamilton County and beyond the I-275 loop for the first time.

2007
Plant capacity increased over 40 percent from 2004, allowing for Ohio wholesale expansion. New strategic alliances formed with Trauth and Smith to expand distribution.

2008
Graeter's introduced to Denver in the first test market without retail, sparking interest from new partners and other markets. Plans begin for new manufacturing plant.

2009
Graeter's breaks ground for its new plant in Bond Hill, to be completed 2010.

2010
Graeter's moves production to new Bond Hill plant and buys out largest franchisee, bringing the total number of company-owned retail stores to twenty-nine.

STORE LOCATIONS

CINCINNATI

Corporate Office/Mount Auburn
2145 Reading Road
Cincinnati, OH 43202
513-721-3323

Cherry Grove
8533 Beechmont Avenue
Cincinnati, OH 45255
513-474-5636

Clifton
332 Ludlow Avenue
Cincinnati, OH 45220
513-281-4749

Deerfield
5076 Natorp Boulevard
Mason, OH 45040
513-339-0140

Finneytown
899 West Galbraith
Cincinnati, OH 45232
513-522-8157

Foutain Square
511 Walnut Street
Cincinnati, OH 45202
513-381-4191

Hyde Park Square
2704 Erie Avenue
Cincinnati, OH 45208
513-321-6221

Kenwood
7369 Kenwood Road
Cincinnati, OH 45236
513-793-5665

Mariemont Square
6918 Wooster Pike
Cincinnati, OH 45227
513-272-0859

Northgate
9356 Colerain Avenue
Cincinnati, OH 45251
513-385-5045

Springdale
11511 Princeton Road
Cincinnati, OH 45246
513-771-7157

Western Hills
2376 Ferguson Road
Cincinnati, OH 45238
513-755-2236

Western Hills
3301 Westbourne Drive
Cincinnati, OH 45248
513-922-8700

COLUMBUS

Corporate Office/Bethel Road
2555 Bethel Road
Columbus, OH 43220
614-442-7622

Bexley
2282 East Main Street
Bexley, OH 43209
614-236-2263

Dublin
6255 Frantz Road
Dublin, OH 43017
614-799-2663

Easton
147 Easton Town Center
Columbus, OH 43219
614-476-2094

Gahanna
425 Beecher Road
Gahanna, OH 43230
614-855-5508

Grove City
4009 Broadway
Grove City, OH 43123
614-277-9011

Pickerington
1500 Cross Creeks Boulevard
Pickerington, OH 43147
614-755-0865

Powell
3762 West Powell Road
Powell, OH 43065
614-336-3661

Upper Arlington
1534 West Lane Avenue
Columbus, OH 43221
614-488-3222

Westerville
1 North State Street
Westerville, OH 43081
614-895-0553

Worthington
654 High Street
Worthington, OH 43085
614-848-5151

DAYTON

Beavercreek
2330-A North Fairfield Road
Beavercreek, OH 45431
937-427-4700

Centerville
2 North Main Street
Centerville, OH 45459
937-312-9001

Oakwood
2412 Far Hills Avenue
Dayton, OH 45419
937-534-0602

Springboro
752 Gardner Road
Springboro, OH 45066
937-748-0300

LEXINGTON

Brighton Place Shoppes
3090 Helmsdale Place
Lexington, KY 40509
859-543-0446

Lexington
325 Romany Road
Lexington, KY 40502
859-543-0446

Palomar
3735 Harrodsburg Road
Lexington, KY 40513
859-296-9636

Tates Creek
4101 Tates Creek Road
Lexington, KY 40517
859-245-4037

LOUISVILLE

Fern Creek
6509 Bardstown Road
Louisville, KY 40291
502-231-2083

Highlands Douglass Loop

2204 Bardstown Road
Louisville, KY 40205
502-451-0044

The Horseshoe Casino Hotel Southern Indiana
11999 Casino Center Drive
Elizabeth, IN 47117
812-969-9100

Landis Lakes
13817 English Villa Drive
Louisville, KY 40245
502-254-1760

New Albany
4310 Charlestown Road
New Albany, IN 47150
812-949-6263

Springhurst
9430 Brownsboro Road
Louisville, KY 40241
502-327-0651

NORTHERN KENTUCKY

Florence
8860 U.S. Highway 42
Florence, KY 41042
859-384-9130

Fort Mitchell

301 Buttermilk Pike
Fort Mitchell, KY 41017
859-781-7770

Newport
1409 North Grand Avenue
Newport, KY 41071
859-781-7770

Newport on the Levee
342 Monmouth Street
Newport, KY 41071
859-261-3160

BIBLIOGRAPHY

Agnew, Ronnie. "Yogurt Challenges Premium Ice Cream." *Cincinnati Enquirer*, October 3, 1988.

Blank Fasig, Lisa. "No Sugar Coating." *Business Courier*, February 6, 2004.

Buckley, Christopher. "Ice Cream: A Memoir." www.forbes.com. June 19, 2006.

Castrodale, Beth. "Graeter's Dips into Ky. Market." *Cincinnati Enquirer*, June 29, 1987.

Chatzky, Jean. "Get the Scoop." *Money*, August 2006.

Cho, Janet. "Pierre's Ice Cream Co. Gets Unanimous Approval for $6 Million Expansion from Cleveland Planning Commission." *Cleveland Plain Dealer*, September 4, 2009.

Cincinnati. "Hometown Foods That Define Our City." June 2004.

Cincinnati Enquirer. "Illness Is Fatal to Mrs. Graeter, Confectioner, 80." December 27, 1955.

Cincinnati Enquirer. "My Lover's a Rover." March 18, 1887.

"Cincinnati–Northern Kentucky Metropolitan Area." www.statemaster.com/encyclopedia/Cincinnati/Northern-Kentucky-metropolitan-area#history.

"Farming in the 40s: Changes in Eating Habits." www.livinghistoryfarm.org/farminginthe40s/life_24.html.

Food Timeline FAQs: Ice Cream & Ice, the Food Timeline. www.foodtimeline.org/foodicecream.html.

Friedman, Brian. "Ice Cream Worth Any Price?" *Cincinnati Enquirer*, September 10, 1983.

"Frozen Yogurt." www.madehow.com/Volume-2/Frozen-Yogurt.html.

Gallagher, Patricia. "Gently, Graeter's Expands." *Cincinnati Enquirer*, March 13, 1989.

———. "Graeter's Sweet on Kroger: Grocery Stores Offer 24-Hour, Year-Round Market." *Cincinnati Enquirer*, March 8, 1990.

Giglierano, Geoffey J., and Deborah A. Overmyer, with Frederic L. Propas. *The Bicentennial Guide to Greater Cincinnati: A Portrait of Two Hundred Years.* Cincinnati, OH: Cincinnati Historical Society, 1988.

Goss, Charles Frederick. *Cincinnati, The Queen City, Volume III.* Cincinnati, OH: 1912.

Gourmet. "It's in the Mail." N.d.

"Ice Cream and Frozen Desserts in the U.S.: Markets and Opportunities in Retail and Foodservice." 6th edition. Packaged Facts January 2010.

"The Influenza Epidemic of 1918." www.archives.gov/exhibits/influenza-epidemic.

Hunter, David. "Dip Duel of '79." *Enquirer Magazine,* August 5, 1979.

Hutton, Punch. "Hot Gifts." *Vanity Fair,* December 2005.

Klein, Dustin S. "A New Flavor." *Smart Business,* February 2005.

Lago, Fred "Chico." *Ben & Jerry's: The Inside Scoop.* New York: Crown Trade Paperbacks, 1995.

Lampert, Eric E. "Dairy Industry." Encyclopedia.com. www.encyclopedia.com/doc/1G2-3401801124.html.

Mattus, Rose Vessel, with Jeanette Friedman. *The Emperor of Ice Cream: The True Story of Häagen-Dazs.* New Milford, NJ: Wordsmithy, 2004.

Moskin, Julia. "Creamy, Healthier Ice Cream? What's the Catch?" *New York Times,* July 26, 2006.

"The 1950s: Lifestyles and Social Trends: Overview." 2001. www.encyclopedia.com/doc/1G2-3468301956.html.

"The 1940s: Lifestyles and Social Trends: Overview." 2001. www.encyclopedia.com/doc/1G2-3468301582.html.

"The 1960s: Lifestyles and Social Trends: Overview." 2001. www.encyclopedia.com/doc/1G2-3468302349.html.

O, The Oprah Magazine. "I Scream, You Scream." July 2002.

Painter, Darin. "Hot Competition in the Freezer Case: Ohio Ice Cream Producers Fight National Brands for Grocery Store Space with Product and Marketing Innovation." *Inside Business,* September 1, 2008.

Phillips, David. "Quality of Quantity." *Dairy Foods,* March 1, 2007.

Pucin, Diane. "Graeter Wins at Tennis, Ice Cream." *Cincinnati Post,* July 27, 1979.

Rosengarten, David. "The Greatest Hits: The 25 Best Products I've Ever Recommended...Revisted!" *Rosengarten Report,* May 5, 2005.

Ruby, Jeff. "A Fork in the Road." *Chicago,* June 2005.

Saveur. "The Saveur 12 Ice Cream Parlors." N.d.

Saveur. "Sweet Stuff." N.d.

Sel, Shawn. "10 Great Places to Scream for Ice Cream." *USA Today,* July 19, 2002.

Siegel, Jim. "Delaware County GOP Endorses Petro for Govenor." *Columbus Dispatch,* June 7, 2005.

Walnut Hills News, May 12, 1882.

"Wars and Battles, The Home Front." www.u-s-history.com/pages/h1764.html.

Wilkerson, Isabel. "Cincinnati Jury Acquits Museum in Mapplethorpe Obscenity Case." *New York Times*, October 6, 1990.

INDEX

R

S

T

U

V

W

ABOUT THE AUTHOR

R obin Davis Heigel has been the food editor at the *Columbus Dispatch* since 2002. She is also the host of *Dispatch Kitchen* cooking segments and specials on the local CBS affiliate, WBNS-TV.

Before coming to Columbus, Davis Heigel was a restaurant critic and food writer for the *San Francisco Chronicle*. She came to San Francisco by way of Los Angeles, where she worked as an assistant editor at *Bon Appetit* magazine.

Davis Heigel has a bachelor of arts in English and psychology from the University of Dayton. She also has an associate's degree in culinary arts from the California Culinary Academy.

Davis Heigel is the author of three books: *Wookie Cookies* (Chronicle Books, 1997), *Infusions* (Chronicle Books, 1998) and *The North Market Cookbook* (American Foodways, 2008).